Up & Running with Your Hard Disk

Up & Running with Your Hard Disk

Klaus M. Rübsam

SAN FRANCISCO • PARIS • DÜSSELDORF • LONDON

Acquisitions Editor: Dianne King
Translator: David J. Clark
Editor: Peter Weverka
Technical Editor: Dan Tauber
Word Processor: Deborah Maizels
Book Designer: Elke Hermanowski
Typesetter: Ingrid Owen
Proofreader: Patsy Owens
Indexer: Nancy Anderman Guenther
Cover Designer: Kelly Archer
Screen reproductions produced by XenoFont

Back-It is a trademark of Gazelle Systems.
Coretest is a trademark of Core International.
Data Pac is a trademark of Tandon Computer Corporation.
DISK MANAGER is a trademark of Ontrack Computer Systems, Inc.
FastBack and FastBack Plus are trademarks of Fifth Generation Systems.
Flashback is a trademark of Overland Data.
IBM PC, IBM PC/2, and PC-DOS are trademarks of International Business Machines.
MS-DOS and OS/2 are trademarks of Microsoft Corporation.
Norton Utilities is a trademark of Peter Norton Computing.
PC Tools Deluxe is a trademark of Central Point Software.
Pdisk is a trademark of Phoenix Technologies.
SpeedStor is a trademark of Storage Dimensions.
UNIX is a trademark of AT&T Bell Laboratories.
XenoFont is a trademark of XenoSoft.
SYBEX is a registered trademark of SYBEX, Inc.
SYBEX is not affiliated with any manufacturer.

Every effort has been made to supply complete and accurate information. However, SYBEX assumes no responsibility for its use, nor for any infringements of patents or other rights of third parties which would result.

Authorized translation from German Language Edition.
Original copyright ©SYBEX-Verlag GmbH 1989.
Translation ©SYBEX Inc. 1990

Library of Congress Card Number: 89-63319
ISBN: 0-89588-666-9
Manufactured in the United States of America
10 9 8 7 6 5 4 3 2 1

Up & Running

Let's say that you are comfortable with your PC. You know the basic functions of word processing, spreadsheets, and database management. In short, you are a committed and eager PC user who would like to gain familiarity with several popular programs as quickly as possible. The Up & Running series of books from SYBEX has been developed for you.

This clearly structured guide shows you in 20 steps what the product can do, how you make it work, and how soon you can achieve practical results.

Your Up & Running book thus satisfies two needs: It describes the program's capabilities, and it lets you quickly get acquainted with the program's operation. This provides valuable help for a purchase decision, along with a 20-step basic course that will give you a solid foundation in the program—even if you're a beginner with scant prior knowledge.

The benefits are plain to see. First, you'll invest in software that meets your needs because, thanks to the appropriate Up & Running book, you know the program's features and limitations. Second, once you purchase the product, you can skip the instruction manual and learn the basics of the program by following the 20 steps.

We have structured the Up & Running books so that the busy user spends little time studying documentation, and the beginner is not burdened with unnecessary text.

A clock shows your work time for each step. This indicates how much time you can expect to spend on each step with your computer.

Clock

Naturally, you'll need much less time if you only read through the steps rather than carrying them out at your computer. You can also save some time by scanning the short marginal notes to find the most important sections within a step.

Three symbols are used to highlight points of special note. These symbols and their meanings are shown below:

Symbols

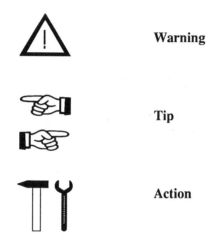

Warning

Tip

Action

An Up & Running book cannot, of course, replace a book or manual containing advanced applications. However, you will receive the information needed to put your hard disk to practical use and to learn basic functions.

Contents

The first step is an overview of the topics discussed in this book. You will find brief explanations of the concepts expanded on in later steps.

The remaining 19 steps discuss discrete aspects of hard disk operations and the variety of hardware and software options available, using examples and short descriptions. Steps 2 through 6 cover hardware, and steps 7 through 19 discuss software. Step 20 is a brief look at upcoming technologies.

An Up & Running book will save you time and money.

SYBEX is very interested in your reaction to the Up & Running series. Your opinions and suggestions will help all of our readers, including yourself.

Preface

Sooner or later everyone who uses a computer needs to know about mass storage media. As computer programs become more and more complex, they produce more data. Storing this data is difficult if you are using a storage medium that was not manufactured to accommodate the new, complex programs.

With so many disks on the market, it is nearly impossible to decide which one will suit your needs. This is especially true if you are not acquainted with the products being offered. Terms such as access time, RLL, ST506, and megabytes are thrown around very casually in product information brochures. This book should provide you with the basic knowledge you need about hard disks so you can make the right decision when you actually purchase one.

I hope that you like the style of this book. It was designed so the reader can learn everything necessary in the shortest amount of time. I would like to thank these firms for the friendly support they gave while I was writing the book: Agora, Seagate, Verbatim, and Western Digital.

Very special thanks go to my wife Petra, for whom, unfortunately, little time was left during the writing of the book. I am very grateful for her patience and endurance.

Klaus Michael Rübsam

Table of Contents

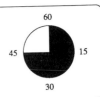
Before you can understand how a hard disk operates, you need to know a few standard terms. Some of these terms are difficult to understand, and so is the technical data concerning hard disks. Still, you have to familiarize yourself with hard disks before you can choose the right one for your needs.

Differences

Not only do hard disks have different storage capacities, but the rate at which they access data is also different. Hard disks differ in appearance, in width (5.25 inches or 3.5 inches), and in height (full- or half-height construction. Their interface with the hard disk controller (ST506, SCSI, ESDI) varies as well.

Similarities

Hard disks are similar in that each is made of round aluminum platters that turn at 3600 revolutions per minute in a hermetically sealed case. Platters are usually double-sided, and each has a 50mm-thick coating of magnetic material. Data is stored in the form of impulse patterns on the magnetic material. Figure 1.1 shows a 3.5-inch hard disk.

A read/write head is located over each aluminum platter in the hard disk. Propelled by the speed of revolution and steered by a stepper motor, the head glides across the surface of the platter at a height of approximately 0.005mm.

Heads

Typically, a personal computer hard disk has a maximum of 16 heads and 16 platters.

Each platter is divided into a series of concentric tracks. Today's technology can produce recording widths of 1000

Tracks

Figure 1.1: A 3.5-inch hard disk

tracks-per-inch (tpi). (High-density floppy disk drives have 98 tpi.) Tracks are numbered from the outside in, beginning with zero.

Sectors

Each track consists of several sectors. Seen from the top, with the tracks of the hard disk layered one on top of the other, the tracks form cylinders.

The number of cylinders and the number of heads varies from hard disk to hard disk. Figure 1.2 shows the connection between platters, tracks, cylinders, and sectors.

Capacity of a Hard Disk

To determine the megabyte capacity of a hard disk, you must have the following information:

- the number of heads
- the number of cylinders
- the number of sectors

Calculating capacity

Hard disk capacity = heads x cylinders x sectors x 512 bytes
(the number of bytes per sector).

Calculating with bytes

Remember that 1024 bytes equals a kilobyte, and 1024 kilobytes equals 1 megabyte. This calculation is made using the binary system, as are most calculations in computer technology.

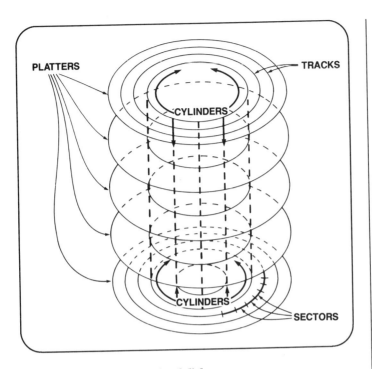

Figure 1.2: The parts of a hard disk

Sometimes the conversion from bytes to kilobytes and mega-bytes is performed in the wrong number system, that is, the calculation is made using 1000, not 1024. This is why manu-facturers and vendors often list different capacities for the same hard disk.

Encoding Schemes

Besides the number of heads and the number of cylinders, hard disk capacity depends on which encoding scheme is used. MFM encoding places 17 sectors on each track, and RLL encoding places 26 sectors on each track. So a hard disk with 615 tracks using the MFM encoding scheme has a capacity of about 20 megabytes, whereas one with 615 tracks using the RLL encoding scheme has a capacity of about 30 megabytes.

ESDI hard disks work with the RLL encoding scheme, but with a maximum data transfer of 10 megabytes. In this way,

36 sectors can be put onto a track.

Hard disk capacities of over 300 megabytes are no longer a rarity. It would take about 850 conventional 360 kilobyte diskettes to equal the storage capacity of one 360 megabyte hard disk.

Why hard disks are faster than diskettes

In contrast to the diskette drive, the hard disk keeps revolving from the moment you turn on your computer. This is why it takes noticeably less time to access data from a hard disk than it does from a diskette drive—the time it takes a diskette drive to reach the right speed of rotation is avoided.

Treat the Hard Disk with Care

Because the heads of the hard disk are separated—even during writing—from the platters by a few thousandths of a millimeter, you must treat a hard disk with care. Jolting or knocking the hard disk while it is operating can make the heads scratch the aluminum platters. This will result in damage to the track over which the head was passing when the jolt occurred. If the head was passing over the track that stores the file allocation table (the file that tells the computer where data is stored on the hard disk), then the file and all the contents of the hard disk will be lost forever.

Transporting a Computer

Preparation for transport

When a computer is being moved you can never rule out the chance of shocks and jolts, but there are ways to lower the risk of data loss. There are two procedures, parking the heads and lifting them.

Parking the Heads

One way to prevent shocks involves positioning the heads over a special track. This track, found in the middle of the disk, is called the park cylinder or park track.

You can use a special program to position the heads on the park cylinder. Programs for parking the hard disk have names like SHUTDOWN, SHIPDISK, PARKDISK, HDPARK, or PARK. Most hard disks come with a parking program.

If a hard disk has 615 cylinders for data recording, it wouldn't work to position the heads on cylinder 616 because part of the heads would still be located over the data cylinders. On the other hand, if the heads were positioned a little further in, they might bump against the mechanical edge of the disk and be damaged.

To protect the heads, the BIOS (basic input/output system) includes a table with a statement concerning the park cylinder. The park program reads this table and positions the heads on the park cylinder. The BIOS is the part of the operating system responsible for handling communications between the computer and its peripherals.

The park cylinder is usually located behind the last cylinder accessible to the operating system—in other words, on the last cylinder where data can be stored. In this position a read/write head cannot come in contact with the surface of the hard disk, and data cannot be lost.

Once the heads have been parked you can turn off the computer and transport it safely. A program to "unpark" the heads isn't necessary, since the BIOS unparks the heads next time the computer is turned on. Some hard disks park their heads automatically when the current is turned off. With these hard disks, a park program would be superfluous.

The heads are usually parked on the outlying directory tracks. When the power is switched off, the heads must travel over the entire disk surface to the park cylinder. This operation makes a light whirring sound. This sound is completely normal and no cause for alarm, but if an unusual noise occurs, it could mean that the hard disk is going to crash soon. In such a case, make a data backup of your files immediately.

Lifting the Head

Another way to avoid damaging the hard disk and the data contained on it is to enlarge the distance between the head and the disk by lifting the head. With this procedure, the head is lowered onto the aluminum disk with a small magnet when the power is on, but when the power is off the head is raised again.

The aluminum disk comes to a standstill when the power is turned off, and then the heads are raised. Likewise, the heads are lowered when the aluminum disk begins to spin. This procedure prevents damage to the aluminum disk and head.

Never Open the Hard Disk Housing

Not only is a hard disk harmed by outside shocks and jolts, opening up the hard disk housing causes harm. In fact, opening up the hard disk housing means the certain end of your hard disk, not to mention the cancellation of the manufacturer's guarantee. Even the smallest dust particle can make the surface of a hard disk unusable during operation. So don't open the housing under any circumstances.

Hard disks are assembled and hermetically sealed in dust-free rooms. To give you an idea of the inner construction of a hard disk, look at Figure 1.3.

MFM and RLL Encoding

You already know that the storage capacity of a hard disk depends largely on which method of data encoding is used, the

Figure 1.3: Opened Seagate hard disk model ST 251

MFM or the RLL scheme. Each hard disk must run under the encoding scheme to which it is suited. A hard disk manufactured for the MFM encoding scheme will not necessarily operate under the RLL scheme.

Nevertheless, hard disks manufactured for the MFM and RLL encoding scheme have only few minor differences. These differences are hard to recognize at first. Hard disks manufactured for RLL have an extra amplifier circuit on the hard disk's controller circuit. This is why there is less background noise with the RLL encoding scheme than there is with the otherwise identically constructed MFM hard disks.

Use hard disks with the RLL encoding scheme only if the hard disk was released solely for that scheme by the manufacturer. Manufacturers give no guarantee for the operational reliability of an MFM hard disk that uses the RLL encoding scheme.

Interface Systems

Another difference between hard disks has to do with the interface and control that is achieved by way of the accompanying hard disk controller. There are three interface systems: the ST506/ST412, SCSI, and ESDI.

Probably the most common system is the ST506/ST412 interface. It consists of a 34-pin cable for disk control—this cable controls drive selection, head selection, etc.—and another 20-pin cable for data. The control cable is connected to all installed hard disks one after the other. This connection method is known as daisy-chaining.

Terminating Resistor

When two hard disks are connected, the resistor circuit of the first hard disk must be disabled. This terminating resistor is usually of the plug-in type. Most often it is located near the 34-pin connection of the hard disk. Refer to the technical manual that came with your hard disk drive for further details about the terminating resistor.

Selection of Hard Disks

Handling a hard disk drive is not advised. Still, if you have to connect a second hard disk to your system, jumpers (plastic-covered electrical connectors) or DIP switches are located on each hard disk drive to select the right drive signals.

Hard disk drives are usually set at the factory as the second disk drive. But a twist in the cable before the second plug makes the hard disk attached to this plug be drive 1, even though it was set to be drive 2. Some cables do not have a twist. In this case, drive 1 should be set to drive 1 and drive 2 should be set to drive 2.

The 20-pin data cable is not daisy-chained; instead, a separate cable is required for each hard disk.

Characteristics of Cable Connections

Colored markings

To make sure you know which cable connects the controller and the hard disk, one side of the cable is distinguished by a colored strip. The colored side is usually connected to pin 1.

In addition, the plug that goes into the hard disk has an extra terminal guard. The terminal guard is there to make sure the connector cable is attached right-side-up. To identify pin 1 on the hard disk controller, a mark appears next to pin 1. The mark can be either the number 1, or a solder mark in the form of a triangle or rectangle.

Marking for pin 1

If you can't find a mark identifying pin 1, you can determine the position of pin 1 with the control and data connection tables below.

The ST506/412 Interface

Tables 1.1 and 1.2 show the typical configuration of the control and data connections of the ST506/412 interface. The signal functions will be discussed later.

Signal Name	Signal Line	Ground Line
Reduced Write Current/		
Head Select 3	2	1
Head Select 2	4	3
Write Gate	6	5
Seek Complete	8	7
Track 0	10	9
Write Fault	12	11
Head Select 0	14	13
Reserved	16	15
Head Select 1	18	17
Index	20	19
Ready	22	21
Step	24	23
Drive Select 1	26	25
Drive Select 2	28	27
Reserved/Drive Select 3	30	29
Reserved/Drive Select 4	32	31
Direction In/		
Direction Select	34	33

Table 1.1: ST506/412 Control Connection

Signal Name	Signal Line
Drive Selected/Reserved	1
Gnd	2
Reserved	3
Gnd	4
Reserved	5
Gnd	6
Reserved	7
Gnd	8
Reserved	9
Reserved	10
Gnd	11
Gnd	12
+MFM/RLL Write Data	13
−MFM/RLL Write Data	14
Gnd	15

Table 1.2 ST506/412 Data Connection

Signal Name	Signal Line
Gnd	16
+MFM/RLL Read Data	17
−MFM/RLL Read Data	18
Gnd	19
Gnd	20

Table 1.2: ST506/412 Data Connection (cont.)

Data Transfer Rates

Differing data transfer rates

The speed at which data travels from the hard disk to the controller is called the data transfer rate. An MFM-encoded hard disk with an ST506/412 connection has a maximum data transfer rate of 5 megabits per second. This corresponds to a maximum data transmittal rate of about 510 kilobytes per second from the computer's controller.

An RLL-encoded hard disk transfers data from the hard disk drive to the controller at an even faster rate: 7.5 megabits per second. This results in a maximum data transmittal rate of about 780 kilobytes per second from the controller to the computer.

The advanced RLL encoding scheme is even faster and functions with a data transfer rate of 9 to 10 megabits per second.

Interleaving

So the computer will have enough time to transfer the data on a sector from the hard disk drive to the corresponding place in main memory, interleaving is used. When this is done, the sectors are not numbered consecutively.

Interleave factor

Instead, sectors are numbered so that the hard disk can read the next logical sector immediately, although the hard disk has already spun further in the meantime. The factor by which sectors are jumped over or left out is called the interleave factor. Interleaving is discussed in more detail in Step 7.

In order to keep the time it takes to read or write to a file as brief as possible, the time it takes to access a sector must also be brief. Manufacturers of slow hard disks seldom give much consideration to the interleave factor. The typical hard disk accesses a sector in about 72 microseconds (ms).

The ESDI Interface

The enhanced small device interface (ESDI) is a further development of the ST506/412 interface. The command protocol of the ESDI interface is noticeably more intelligent than that of the ST506/412 interface.

The data transfer rate of the ESDI interface is between 10 and 15 megabits per second. The ESDI hard disk connector configuration is slightly different from the ST506/412 configuration, and the ST506/412 configuration can't be operated with an ESDI controller. Another disadvantage of the ESDI controller is its very high price.

Tables 1.3 and 1.4 show the typical configuration of the control and data connections of the ESDI interface.

In contrast to the ST506/412 interface, the connector cable between the ESDI interface and the hard disk may not have a twist.

No cable twist

Signal Name	*Signal Line*	*Ground Line*
Head Select 3	2	1
Head Select 2	4	3
Write Gate	6	5
Config/Status Data	8	7
Transfer ACK	10	9
Attention	12	11
Head Select 0	14	13
Sector	16	15
Head Select 1	18	17
Index	20	19
Ready	22	21
Transfer Request	24	23
Drive Select 1	26	25

Table 1.3: ESDI Control Connection

Signal Name	Signal Line	Ground Line
Drive Select 2	28	27
Drive Select 3	30	29
Read Gate	32	31
Command Data	34	33

Table 1.3: ESDI Control Connection (cont.)

Signal Name	Signal Line
Drive Selected	1
Sector	2
Command Complete	3
Address Mark Enable	4
Reserved	5
Gnd	6
+Write Clock	7
−Write Clock	8
Reserved	9
+Read/Reference Clock	10
−Read/Reference Clock	11
Gnd	12
+NRZ Write Data	13
−NRZ Write Data	14
Gnd	15
Gnd	16
+NRZ Read Data	17
−NRZ Read Data	18
Gnd	19
Index	20

Table 1.4: ESDI Data Connection

The SCSI Interface

Maximum of eight devices

Hard disks with the small computer system interface (SCSI) connection have a data transfer rate of 10 or 15 megabits per second. The advantage of the SCSI connection lies in its architecture. With its data bus and its nine additional control lines, the SCSI connection allows up to eight devices to be connected to a hard disk. In other words, data can be shared among eight devices.

In addition, streamer tape drives or other devices with SCSI connections can be driven together with hard disks on one controller. There are two methods of driving the SCSI devices: synchronously and asynchronously. In the asynchronous method, up to 1.5 megabytes per second can be transmitted; with the synchronous method as much as 4 megabytes per second can be transmitted. SCSI hard disks can achieve an effective data transmittal rate of about 750 kilobytes per second. Table 1.5 shows the configuration of the SCSI interface.

Extremely fast data transmittal

Signal Name	Signal Line	Ground Line
D0	2	1
D1	4	3
D2	6	5
D3	8	7
D4	10	9
D5	12	11
D6	14	13
D7	16	15
DBP	18	17
Reserved	20	19
Reserved	22	21
Reserved	24	23
TPWR (Terminator Power)	26	25
Reserved	28	27
Reserved	30	29
ATN	32	31
Reserved	34	33
BSY	36	35
ACK	38	37
RST	40	39
MSG	42	41
SEL	44	43

Table 1.5: 50-pin SCSI Interface Connection

Signal Name	Signal Line	Ground Line
C/D	46	45
REQ	48	47
I/O	50	49

Table 1.5: 50-pin SCSI Interface Connection (cont.)

Like hard disks with ST506/412 connections, SCSI devices have a resistor circuit (a terminating resistor), usually a plug-in type. If two SCSI hard disks are attached, the terminating resistor must be removed from the first hard disk. In fact, the terminating resistor has to be removed from all peripheral devices except the last. Refer to the technical manual that came with your hard disk for more information about terminology resistors. Figure 1.4 shows some hard disks with SCSI connections.

Figure 1.4: Seagate hard disks with SCSI connections

Step 2:

Data Encoding

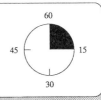

Independent of the hard disk, three data encoding schemes are available—MFM, RLL, and Advanced RLL. These encoding schemes transform the serial bitstream—a continuous stream of bits—into charges of magnetic flux on the surface of the hard disk. The hard disk controller perceives only one flux reversal, in other words, one fluctuation of the magnetization. This doesn't suffice, depending on the state of the bits at this point, to magnetize the hard disk in one direction or the other. In effect, only flux reversals—changes in the polarity—are processed by the hard disk controller.

Various data encoding schemes

MFM Encoding Scheme

The most common hard disk encoding scheme is modified frequency modulation (MFM). With MFM, the hard disk revolves at a constant rate and data is transferred likewise at an unchanging rate. This means that each bit transferred from the controller to the hard disk is, in a physical sense, available in the same place on the hard disk. Figure 2.1 shows a MFM hard disk controller.

When a data bit being transferred from the controller to the hard disk has the value 1, it produces a magnetization in one or the other direction exactly in the middle of the field reserved for this information bit.

When a 0 is being transferred, it produces a brief change in the flux density at the very beginning of the field. But if a 1 is encoded in the previous field, no change in the field occurs. So a series of zeros looks like a series of ones—they differentiate themselves solely in the phase location.

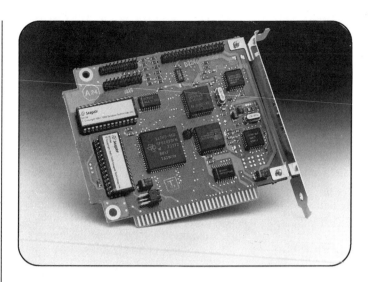

Figure 2.1: MFM hard disk controller for the XT ST11M

RLL Encoding Scheme

Run-length limited (RLL) is another encoding scheme. Sometimes this encoding scheme is called RLL 2.7.

Increase in capacity

With RLL, groups of several bits are combined and converted into a new code with variable length. In this way, the bit density of the hard disk is tripled. Through the recoding process, however, the number of bits is doubled. The available capacity of RLL hard disks with the ST506/412 connection is around 50 percent. Instead of having the usual 17 sectors that an MFM hard disk has, RLL hard disks have 26 sectors per track. This produces a capacity of 13 kilobytes for every track, making the RLL data transfer rate climb about 50 percent to 7.5 megabits per second. An RLL-encoded hard disk with the ESDI interface can have a maxium of 36 sectors per track, which results in a capacity of up to 18 kilobytes per track.

Data safety

Error Correction

In order to guarantee data safety despite the high density of information, more elaborate error correction algorithms are used with the RLL encoding scheme than with the MFM scheme. But to use the RLL data encoding scheme you must have a drive suitable for RLL. Figure 2.2 shows an RLL hard disk.

Figure 2.2: An ST238R RLL hard disk

Advanced RLL

The Advanced RLL encoding scheme increases disk capacity by 90 percent over the "normal" MFM-encoded hard disks. A hard disk with 615 cylinders and four heads has a capacity of 39 megabytes with the Advanced RLL encoding scheme. Besides that, the data transfer rate increases to 9 megabits per second.

90 percent more

Advanced RLL has even more thorough error correction measures than RLL does, so it can be used on a wider range of hard disks.

Before you purchase an Advanced RLL controller, find out if the drive you will connect it to is Advanced-RLL compatible.

In conclusion, a brief review:

MFM:

modified frequency method; data transfer rate is 5 megabits per second

RLL (2.7):

run-length limited; 50 percent greater capacity relative to MFM (with ST506/412 interface); the data transfer rate is 7.5 megabits per second or 10 megabits per second (with an ESDI interface)

Advanced RLL:

advanced run-length limited; 90 percent greater capacity relative to MFM; the data transfer rate is 9 megabits per second

Step 3:

Choosing a Hard Disk

Selecting Hard Disks

Taking into consideration hard disk technology and the capacity requirements of mass storage, it is difficult to decide which hard disk to buy.

Which Hard Disk Is the Right One?

There are internal hard disks, external hard disks, plug-in hard disks that attach to a slot in the computer, as well as cartridges, which are accessible from the outside and therefore can be removed from the computer easily when the need arises.

For personal use, a hard disk with a capacity of 20 or 30 megabytes is perfectly sufficient.

With so many programs being offered nowadays, and with programs growing in size, it is very easy to fill the hard disk with programs. But try to keep only programs and data you truly need on your hard disk. This way you will always have enough room for your programs. Store programs that you seldom use on diskettes—you'll save space on your hard disk this way.

A Second Hard Disk

If there is already a hard disk in the computer and you want to install another one, you will likely have to use the same type of interface and encoding scheme established by the existing controller. But if this isn't the case, you must decide which interface and encoding scheme to use. Refer to the distinctions made between the individual systems in Steps 1 and 2 to reach a decision.

Hard Disk Construction

Full-height 5.25-inch hard disks have an installed depth of about 203 mm, a width of 149 mm, and a height of 86 mm. Half-height 5.25-inch hard disks have a height of only 43 mm. A 3.5-inch hard disk has a depth of about 150 mm, a width of 105 mm, and a height of 44 mm.

Plug-in hard disks are attached to the associated controller in a single unit and fit into an 8-bit slot in the computer. They have to be installed in older PCs, since older PCs already have two full-height diskette drives and there isn't enough room for a conventional hard disk drive.

Most external hard disks have a SCSI interface. This interface allows shielded cables up to 6 meters long.

Cartridges

Some computer manufacturers offer cartridges with their computers. You can place a cartridge in an insertion slot constructed for that purpose and eject the cartridge again—after the heads of the hard disk are positioned on the park cylinder—when you're done working. Cartridges are ideal for storing data that must be protected against unauthorized access. You can store the cartridge in a secure place where no one can get to it.

Once you've decided on the construction method, interface type, and encoding scheme, you can start comparing the other technical data of the hard disks in question. Last but not least, the price will play a decisive role when you choose which hard disk to buy.

Reduced Write Current

In some hard disks the write current—the current that goes through the write head and transfers data to the hard disk—is reduced to a lower level. Disks of this kind are said to have reduced write current (RWC). Reducing the write current is done to keep data on a single track: a powerful write current might cause data to write over more than one track at a time. Reduced write current usually occurs toward the center of the disk, where the tracks are closer together.

Reducing the write current is usually handled by the controller, but on hard disks with more than 8 heads, the hard disk drive itself takes over control of the write current. On hard disk drives with more than 8 heads, the control lines otherwise reserved for reducing the write current are reassigned the task of head selection, which is why the hard disk drive must control the write current.

Write Pre-Compensation

Because cylinders become smaller the closer they are to the center of the hard disk, and because this results in a decrease in relative speed, the write data must be recorded with a time delay of about 10–12 nanoseconds on cylinders close to the center of the disk. This procedure is called write pre-compensation (WPC). Write pre-compensation is used, if at all, only with MFM-encoded hard disks.

WPC

Used Hard Disks

There is nothing wrong with buying a used personal computer, but under no circumstances should you consider buying a used hard disk. One can examine used cars from the inside and the outside, but this can't be done with hard disks.

New Hard Disks with Defects

Most new hard disks already have defective tracks, but this is nothing to worry about as long as the number of defective tracks stays within certain limits. In fact, defective tracks are not a sign of an inferior hard disk. Hard disks with defective tracks aren't necessarily worse than hard disks without them.

Don't worry about defective tracks

Each hard disk is tested for defects by the manufacturer. Not only are permanent defects located, but so are intermittent, or soft defects.

Defects discovered in these tests are recorded on a defect list, or defect map. You'll find this list or map affixed to the outside of the hard disk or on an accompanying computer printout.

You must tell your computer where the defective tracks are during the low-level formatting stage. The manufacturer has already figured in defects, and this is why hard disks are said to have a guaranteed minimum capacity. To find out minimum capacity, give the "CHKDSK C:" command in DOS. Your computer will display a message telling you how many bytes are in bad sectors—in this way you'll know how much the capacity of your hard disk has been reduced. If you forget to specify where defective tracks are during the low-level formatting stage, you might write data onto defective tracks. Moreover, you have to specify defective tracks during low-level formatting—you have to use a special utility to specify defective tracks if you try to do so after the computer becomes functional. Your computer will report defective tracks you forgot to specify by displaying the "Error reading drive C" message in DOS.

Step 4:

Controllers

Which interface a hard disk uses is a crucial consideration in the selection of the right controller. There are three interfaces to choose from:

- the ST506/412 interface
- the ESDI interface
- the SCSI interface

Each type of hard disk only has one acceptable interface. Nevertheless, you can choose between two kinds of controllers, one with an 8-bit bus (for PCs, XTs, and ATs) and one with a 16-bit bus (for the AT or 386). Furthermore, you can get controller cards to which you can attach two diskette drives in addition to two hard disk drives. These controllers are referred to as combo-controllers.

XT controllers come with their own BIOS for controlling the hard disk, so XT controllers can be installed in computers of the XT class. These XT controllers can also be installed in AT computers and 386 machines.

Control-lers with BIOS for hard disk control

If the controller includes a BIOS, you must enter 0 as the number of installed hard disks.

With ATs, a special BIOS on the controller card is not absolutely necessary. ATs already have a table in their BIOS where hard disk specifications—the number of heads, park cylinder location, and several other specifications—are contained.

SETUP Program

AT and 386 computers have a special SETUP program either in ROM or on a separate diskette. SETUP programs allow you to select drives of various sizes. You select one by entering a number corresponding to the drive you want. The number you enter is stored in CMOS RAM.

Because CMOS RAM and the real-time clock are battery-driven, the drive number you enter is retained when you turn off your computer. With the Expanded Diagnostics Diskette from IBM, for instance, the drive number is entered in the CMOS RAM of the AT (Figure 4.1). You use the same procedure to enter the drive number on 386 computers.

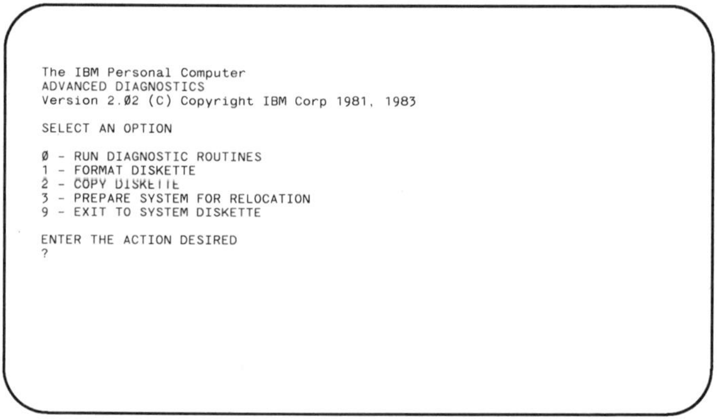

```
The IBM Personal Computer
ADVANCED DIAGNOSTICS
Version 2.02 (C) Copyright IBM Corp 1981, 1983

SELECT AN OPTION

0 - RUN DIAGNOSTIC ROUTINES
1 - FORMAT DISKETTE
2 - COPY DISKETTE
3 - PREPARE SYSTEM FOR RELOCATION
9 - EXIT TO SYSTEM DISKETTE

ENTER THE ACTION DESIRED
?
```

Figure 4.1: The opening menu of the IBM PC Advanced Diagnostics

Other computer manufacturers provide comparable programs for the ATs that come with their computers.

With many ATs, however, there are no choices provided for RLL-encoded hard disk drives, which have a higher number of sectors per track. In order to run an RLL-encoded hard disk on such an AT, proceed as follows:

1. Ascertain the sum of the formatting sectors on the RLL hard disk. Do this by multiplying the number of heads by the number of cylinders by the number of sectors. The outcome is usually 26.

2. Enter this information in the AT BIOS table. The hard disk type found in the AT BIOS table with the same or next

smallest number of sectors will be entered in the CMOS RAM of the AT.

3. The rest is taken care of by a special program for initializing the RLL hard disk. This program asks for the actual number of heads, cylinders, and sectors to be formatted. Later the RLL controller will recalculate these specfications with every access of the hard disk. This translation procedure is called translate mode.

Controllers for RLL-encoded hard disks often have their own BIOS for driving the hard disk. In this case, you must enter "no hard disk" or "type 0" as the hard disk type in the CMOS RAM.

8/16-Bit Controllers

In ATs, a 16-bit controller is preferable to an 8-bit controller because of its higher data throughput. This is because a 16-bit controller transmits at twice the speed of an 8-bit controller.

Controllers for IBM PS/2s

Computers of the IBM PS/2 series require special controllers, unless they come with built-in controllers in the first place. The WD1007V-MC1 controller from Western Digital, for instance, was designed specifically for use in computers with microchannel architecture.

On this controller, which was made to be installed in the IBM PS/2 50, 60, 80, or compatible machines, two ESDI hard disk drives can be operated. In order to attach an MFM- or RLL-encoded hard disk with the ST506/412 interface to these computers, the WD1006V-MC1 controller, also from Western Digital, must be installed.

The following overviews represent a selection of the controller cards available on the market.

The ST506/412 Interface System

Data Encoding Scheme: MFM

XT Controllers:

ACB2010A	(contains BIOS for hard disk control)
DTC5150CRH	(contains BIOS for hard disk control)
LCS6210	(contains BIOS for hard disk control)
NCL5427	(contains BIOS for hard disk control)
OMTI5520B-10	(contains BIOS for hard disk control)
WD1002A-WX1	(contains BIOS for hard disk control)
WDXT-GEN	(contains BIOS for hard disk control)
WDXT-GEN2	(contains BIOS for hard disk control)

AT Controllers:

LCS6610
NCL5426
OMTI8140
WD1002-WAH
WD1003-WAH
WD1003V-MM1
WD1003V-SM1
WD1006V-MM1
WD1006V-SM1   (1:1 Interleave)

AT Combo-Controllers:

DTC5280(–2)
LCS6620
MORSE AT-2000
NCL5125
NCL5425
OMTI8240
WD1002-WA2
WD1003-WA2
WD1003V-MM2
WD1003V-SM2
WD1006V-MM2
WD1006V-SM2   (1:1 Interleave)

Microchannel Controller:

WD1006V-MC1

Data Encoding Scheme: RLL 2.7

XT Controllers:

ACB2072	(contains BIOS for hard disk control)
DTC5160CRH	(contains BIOS for hard disk control)
NCL5227	(contains BIOS for hard disk control)
OMTI5527B-10	(contains BIOS for hard disk control)
WD1002A-27X	(contains BIOS for hard disk control)
WDXT-GEN2R	(translate mode, contains BIOS for hard disk control)

AT Controllers:

OMTI8147	(translate mode)
WD1003-RAH	(translate mode)
WD1003S-RAH	(translate mode)
WD1003V-SR1	(contains BIOS for hard disk control)
WD1006V-SR1	(contains BIOS for hard disk control)

AT Combo-Controllers:

ACB2372	(contains BIOS for hard disk control)
DTC5287(–2)	(contains BIOS for hard disk control)
NCL5225	(contains BIOS for hard disk control)
OMTI8247	(contains BIOS for hard disk control)
WD1003-RA2	(translate mode)
WD1003A-RA2	(translate mode)
WD1003V-SR2	(contains BIOS for hard disk control)

Microchannel Controller:

WD1006V-MCR

Data Encoding Scheme: Advanced RLL

XT Controllers:

Perstor PS-180   (contains BIOS for hard disk control)

AT Controllers:

ACB2382   (contains BIOS for hard disk control)

The ESDI Interface System

Data Encoding Scheme: ESDI

AT Controllers:

WD1005-WAH   (contains BIOS for hard disk control)
WD1007A-WAH   (contains BIOS for hard disk control)
WD1007V-SE1   (contains optional BIOS for hard disk control)

AT Combo-Controllers:

ACB2322   (contains BIOS for hard disk control)
WD1007A-WA2   (contains BIOS for hard disk control)
WD1007V-SE1   (contains optional BIOS for hard disk control)

OMTI8620   This controller also has an ST506/412 interface for operation with MFM-encoded hard disk drives.

OMTI8627   This controller also has an ST506/412 interface for operation with RLL-encoded hard disk drives.

Microchannel Controller:

WD1007V-MC1

SCSI Interface System with Host Adapter

Data Encoding Scheme: Hard Disk Dependent
MFM or RLL 2.7

XT Host Adapters:

Future Domain TMC830
Seagate ST01   (only for Seagate hard disks)
WDSCS-ATXT

XT Combo-Controller/Host Adapter:

Seagate ST02   (only for Seagate hard disks)

AT Host Adapters:

Rodime AT Adapter   (only for Rodime hard disks)
WD7000-ASC   (contains BIOS for hard disk
                      control; optional with floppy disk
                      controller)

AT Combo-Controller/Host Adapter:

Future Domain TMC87   (contains BIOS for hard disk control)

Microchannel Host Adapter:

WD7000-MSC

Figure 4.2 shows a SCSI host adaptor for XT computers.

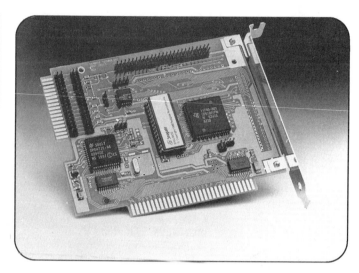

Figure 4.2: SCSI Host adapter ST02 for XT computers

Step 5:

Accessories

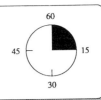

You should investigate a few important matters before you install your hard disk and make it operational.

Adequate Power

The first and most important thing to establish is whether the power supply of the computer has sufficient reserve wattage to operate a hard disk. A power supply of 150 watts is almost always adequate. Only consider a higher wattage power supply if you have an older machine outfitted with a 90-watt power supply. This way you avoid unwanted surprises. The wattage requirement of a hard disk depends on its technical specifications. A Seagate ST225, for example, has a wattage requirement of 14.8 watts.

Sufficient reserve wattage available

If the power supply should prove to have no more free power connectors, you can purchase a power fork cable, also called a T-piece. This cable is attached, for instance, between the power supply and the diskette drive. The remaining end is plugged into the power connection of the hard disk.

The asymmetrical plug on the power supply connectors is there to guard against short circuits. Never force the 4-pin plug into the corresponding socket on the hard disk.

Mechanical polarity guard

Connector Cables

Two more cables are needed: a 20-pin data cable and a 34-pin control cable. The control cable in your computer might already be constructed to accommodate an extra hard disk. Both cables must have a male plug and a female plug with flat contacts at either end. There might be two female plugs to accommodate two hard disks.

Mounting Materials

In order to install the hard disk drive in your computer you need mounting materials. Depending on your computer, these could be mounting racks with screws. For the tower housings, four screws are usually all that is necessary.

It is a good idea to use a 5.25-inch installation frame to install a 3.5-inch hard disk. Ask your dealer how to do this.

Copy of the Operating System

Use the DOS DISKCOPYcommand to make copies of the operating system diskettes. Label them like the originals and store them in a safe place. This way you'll have a backup copy.

Special Installation Software

Some hard disk controllers or hard disks are shipped with special installation software. For instance, Ontrack offers DISK MANAGER and Storage Dimensions offers Speedstor. Follow the manufacturer's instructions carefully for installing hard disk drives and controllers.

DEBUG is recommended for XT computers

You need the DEBUG progam to install a hard disk in an XT. This program should be on your operating system diskette.

To install a hard disk drive in an AT, the SETUP program is required. In some computers, this program is already contained in the BIOS. Ontrack's DISK MANAGER program and Storage Dimensions' SpeedStor program can also be used to install a hard disk on an AT.

But if you only have the Advanced Diagnostics diskette from IBM, you also need the BASIC program for determining the type number for AT computers (see Figure 5.1). It gives you the various hard disk types supported by your computer's BIOS.

If you can't find a corresponding hard disk type number in the computer BIOS, select the hard disk type with the same number of heads, the same number of sectors per track, and the next

```
10 DEF SEG=&HF000
20 SCREEN 0:WIDTH 80:CLS:KEY OFF
30 PRINT"Program to display hard disk
   types in the AT BIOS"
40 PRINT
50 IF PEEK(&HFFFE)<>252 THEN BEEP:PRINT
   "This computer is not an AT":END
60 L=0
70 FOR TYPE = 0 TO 46:ADR%=TYPE*16+&HE401
80 IF L>0 THEN 120
90 PRINT
100 PRINT"Type Cylinder  Heads  Sectors
    Park-Cylinder  WPC off track  Capacity
    in Mbytes"
110 PRINT"─────────────────────
    ────────────────────"
120 IF PEEK(ADR%)=0 THEN 210
130 L=L+1
140 CYL=PEEK(ADR%)+256*PEEK(ADR%+1)
150 HEAD=PEEK(ADR%+2)
160 PARK=PEEK(ADR%+12)+256*PEEK(ADR%+13)
170 WPC=PEEK(ADR%+5)+256*PEEK(ADR%+6)
180 SEC=PEEK(ADR%+14)
190 CAPA=(PEEK(ADR%)+PEEK(ADR%+1)*256)
    *PEEK(ADR%+2)*SEC*512/(1024*1024)
200 PRINT USING"##       ####      ##
    ## ####    ######
    ###.#";TYPE+1,CYL,HEAD,SEC,PARK,WPC,
    CAPA
210 IF L<20 THEN 260
220 PRINT"Press any key to continue"
230 A$=INKEY$
240 IF A$="" THEN 230
250 L=0
260 NEXT TYPE
270 END
```

Figure 5.1: BASIC program for determining the type number for AT computers

smallest number of tracks. Doing it this way, however, means a portion of your hard disk will never be used. With the DISK MANAGER or SpeedStor program, though, hard disk types not listed by your computer's BIOS can be used without any limitations.

Mounting Location

Always hold your hard disk only by the frame. This way you avoid damage caused by static charges.

Observe the manufacturer's specifications

Observe the manufacturer's specifications when you mount your hard disk. Horizontal, with the circuit board face down, is the most common mounting technique. Yet a vertical mounting on one side is also allowed. Don't mount the hard disk with the short ends upward or downward, though, because if you do the heads will not remain in their last position after you turn off the power.

Bad track map

Step 6 describes how to make the hard disk operational. Meanwhile, look at the bad track map that either came attached to the outside of your hard disk or was provided on a computer printout. If this list is not a computer printout, copy down the table from the sticker on the hard disk now. Note in tabular order each defective head and defective cylinder.

Step 6:

Installation

So far you have been learning theory, but now it is time to put what you've learned into practice. Nevertheless, you should keep some rules of the game in mind. Before you install and connect devices to the computer, make sure the computer is unplugged.

Pull the Plug Out of the Outlet

Disconnect all the cables between your computer and its peripherals—the monitor, printer, and the keyboard. It is much easier to get at the computer without any wires getting in the way.

On most machines you have to remove five screws before you can open the computer's chassis. These screws, located on the back of the computer, hold the two halves of the chassis together. One screw is on the bottom left, one is on the top left, one is in the middle on the top, one is on the top right, and one is on the bottom right. Unfortunately, it is easy to mistake the chassis screws for those of the power supply.

Opening the chassis

Before the upper half of the chassis can be pulled toward the front, the key lock must be in the open, or unlocked position.

Key lock unlocked

Now you must decide exactly where to mount the hard disk. Usually there are two available places. If you want, you can remove the plate covering the slot: choose this place if you intend to add a second diskette drive later on. You should mount the hard disk drive so that if you mount a second floppy drive you don't have to mount the hard disk in another place. This is why it is better to select a location that is fully enclosed in the chassis. Make certain that the jumper, or short-circuit plug is installed correctly. Reswitching it later often involves removing the hard disk.

If you are installing two or more hard disks, remove all but one of the terminating resistor packs. Re-examine the jumpers on the hard disk controller. With XT hard disk controllers, the type of hard disk drive connected must already be set at this point. You will find a table for this purpose in your hard disk controller's documentation.

ST506/412 and ESDI Interface

Locate
pin 1

Examine the 34-pin cable that attaches the hard disk to the controller. On one end there is a 34-pin plug. You connect this side of the cable to the controller. On the controller card there is a mark that tells you where pin 1 is located—the numeral 1, a small triangle by pin 1, or a slightly larger solder point. Be sure to connect the first pin of the 34-pin plug with pin 1 on the controller.

To make it easier to identify the corresponding wire of the 34-pin control cable, the outermost wire is a different color, usually red or blue.

At the other end of the cable there are one or two female plugs with flat contacts. These plugs have an obstruction on the side where pin 1 is located, between pins 3 and 4 and pins 5 and 6. The obstruction is there so you can't connect the hard disk the wrong way around. If your cable has two female plugs and some of the wires are twisted, connect the outtermost plug—the one after the twist—to your hard disk. The remaining middle plug of the control cable is reserved for a second hard disk.

In order to guarantee the correct control of the hard disks, both hard disks must have their jumper pins set for number 2 (DS2: Drive Select 2). Using a cable without a twist, the first hard disk must be selected as number 1. In other words, set your first hard disk to number 1 if you're connecting with an unswitched cable.

Connect the 20-pin data cable the same way as the 34-pin cable, by paying attention to where pin 1 is located both on the controller side and on the hard disk side. On most hard disk controllers, the data cable for the first hard disk drive is next to the control cable shared by both hard disk drives.

Follow the directions of the manufacturer

In the handbook accompanying your hard disk you will find more detailed directions for connecting the 20- and 34-pin cables.

SCSI Interface

Before you install the SCSI hard disk, set the hard disk to an unused address. If this is the first SCSI device begin installed, use address 1. (The host adapter has address 0.)

Setting the SCSI address

Connecting the SCSI hard disk with the host adapter requires a single 50-pin cable. At both ends of the cable there is a 50-pin male plug. Look for the position of pin 1 to find out which of the two plugs is connected to the controller.

To make it easier to identify the corresponding wire of the 50-pin control cable, the outermost wire is marked with a different color, usually red or blue, just like the data cable is. The second plug is attached to the hard disk. Look for the position of pin 1 here as well.

It may be the case that you have to install two mounting rails with your hard disk. In this case, unscrew the two fastening tabs (1 cm × 2 cm) on the computer chassis before you slide in the hard disk unit. Then insert the hard disk into the computer chassis. Now screw in the two fastening tabs to ensure a tight fit.

With all other hard disks, the hard disk is fastened to the chassis with four side screws. The mechanical installation of the hard disk is now finished.

Plug the controller into a slot on the computer

Now you must plug the controller, or host adapter, into an empty slot on the computer. In order to plug in the card, remove one of the narrow plates at the back of the chassis. You must remove one screw to do this. Now carefully insert the card in the slot on your computer. Fasten the card in with the screw so that the card doesn't come loose.

Light Diode for Hard Disk Access

If your computer is already equipped with a control light diode to signal hard disk access, the free plug (2- or 4-pinned) must be attached to the corresponding connecting prongs on the controller card.

Unfortunately, this plug doesn't have an obstruction to guard against plugging it in backwards, so advice can't be made regarding the right connection. An incorrect connection will not cause any damage to the light diode or the controller.

If the light diode doesn't light up during hard disk access, the plug must be reversed on the connecting prongs. Before you screw the chassis of your computer back together, check to see that the light diode functions correctly.

Power Connection

Finally, you must connect your hard disk to your computer's power supply. Plug the 4-pinned power cable plug into the receptacle designed for that purpose on your hard disk. The plug was designed to make it impossible to insert it backwards.

Step 7:

Initialization

Put all the required tools to the side and calmly re-examine the connections between the hard disk and controller card to make sure they fit correctly. Connect your computer, monitor, and keyboard, and plug the computer back into the power outlet as well. Turn off the power and check all the electrical connections once more if you have any doubt that your computer system is running properly.

Now turn on your computer. You shouldn't hear any noises except for the sound of a running motor. If you do hear other noises, or if you have any doubt that your computer is functioning right, turn it off and check all your electrical connections again.

If you have an XT or an AT with an XT hard disk controller, you will receive an error message a moment after you turn on your computer. This error message is completely normal. It appears because your hard disk has not yet been initialized. Initialize means to format a hard disk. (Initialization is sometimes called low-level formatting.)

XT Hard Disk Controllers

Unfortunately, all initialization programs do not follow the same procedures. As a rule, the XT initialization program is contained on the controller card. It is started from the debugger. The starting address is almost always C800:5.

Follow the prompts and directions of the initialization program. You will find instructions about this program in the handbook that came with your hard disk controller. Figure 7.1 shows the opening screen of the XT-GEN Dynamic Formatter initialization program.

```
A>debug
-g=c8ØØ:5


            XT-GEN Dynamic Formatter Rev.1.Ø
   (C) Copyright Western Digital Corp. 1987. Current Drive is C:
            Select new Drive or RETURN for current
```

Figure 7.1: XT-GEN Dynamic Formatter Rev. 1.0

Provide technical data

Some initialization programs require you to provide information about the physical characteristics of your hard disk. You will find this information in a table in the reference manual that came with your hard disk.

Interleave

The interleave gives the shift between physical and logical sectors. As a rule of thumb, the smaller the interleave value, the higher the transmission speed between hard disk and computer. With XTs, you should select an interleave of 5. Utility programs like CORETEST can give you the optimal interleave for your hard disk.

Although 5 is a useful value, ESDI controllers have an interleave factor of 1; that is, no translation between physical and logical sectors takes place. This creates an optimal data transmission speed.

To clarify the interleave shift, the connection between physical and logical sectors is displayed in Table 7.1.

		Interleave factor							
		1	2	3	4	5	6	7	8
	0	0	0	0	0	0	0	0	0
	1	1	2	3	4	5	6	7	8
	2	2	4	6	8	10	12	14	16
	3	3	6	9	12	15	1	1	1
	4	4	8	12	16	1	7	8	9
physical sector	5	5	10	15	1	6	13	15	2
	6	6	12	1	5	11	2	2	10
	7	7	14	4	9	16	8	9	3
	8	8	16	7	13	2	14	16	11
	9	9	1	10	2	7	3	3	4
	10	10	3	13	6	12	9	10	12
	11	11	5	16	10	3	15	4	5
	12	12	7	2	14	8	4	11	13
	13	13	9	5	3	13	10	5	6
	14	14	11	8	7	4	16	12	14
	15	15	13	11	11	9	5	6	7
	16	16	15	14	15	14	11	13	15

Table 7.1: Interleave Factor

Landing Zone, Park Cylinder

Another piece of information the initialization program will need is the location of the landing zone, or park cylinder to which the head should be moved when the hard disk is parked.

Reduced Write Current (RWC)

The initialization program will also need to know about the cylinder at which the write current should be reduced.

Write Pre-Compensation Cylinder (WPC)

The initialization program will also need to know the cylinder number from which write pre-compensation should begin. Write pre-compensation, as well as park cylinders and reduced write current, were described in Step 3.

Finally, the initialization program will prompt you for the number of cylinders and the number of heads on your disk. Follow the instructions of the hard disk manufacturer to answer all these questions.

 With many controllers, no further information is required of the user besides the drive specification. With these controllers, the data is determined by corresponding jumper pin settings.

AT Hard Disk Controllers

The two most common programs used for initializing hard disks are DISK MANAGER and SpeedStor. Each program is discussed below.

DISK MANAGER

Device driver

The DISK MANAGER program, which comes from Ontrack Computer Systems, is shipped together with the DISKPARK program for parking hard disks, the DIAG diagnostic program, and also the DMDRVR.BIN device driver. The DMDRVR.BIN device driver is designed for hard disks with a storage capacity of more than 32 megabytes and a DOS version before 3.3. With hard disks from Seagate, the DISK MANAGER package comes with all hard disks whose storage capacity is greater than 32 megabytes.

There are two ways to start the DISK MANAGER program, either automatically or manually. To run the program automatically, log onto the A drive and enter

        dm

 without specifying any additional parameters. The program will initialize, partition, and install the operating system by itself. Only select automatic installation if you have a hard disk with a capacity of more than 32 megabytes and you wish to install a DOS version before 3.3. In all other cases, you should select the manual installation procedure.

You call up the manual installation procedure by logging onto the A drive and typing

```
dm /m
```

Next, you must modify the CMOS RAM configuration of the computer so that the computer will know that a hard disk is attached and what type of hard disk it is. Figure 7.2 shows the opening screen of the DISK MANAGER program. The first question asks if you want to change the CMOS configuration. Press Y for yes.

Modify CMOS RAM

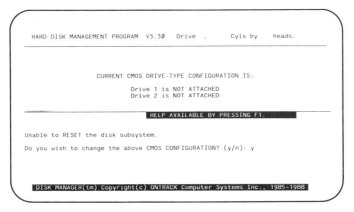

Figure 7.2: Opening screen of the DISK MANAGER program

Next you see the screen in Figure 7.3. This screen applies to the AT controller, the most commonly undertaken installation. Enter the number of hard disks connected to your controller.

The next screen, shown in Figure 7.4, asks for your hard disk type. Because the hard disk drive connected is not from Seagate, press return at the MODEL CODE prompt.

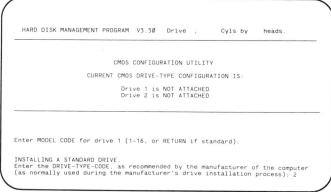

```
HARD DISK MANAGEMENT PROGRAM  V3.3Ø    Drive  ,      Cyls by     heads.

                    CMOS CONFIGURATION UTILITY

              CURRENT CMOS DRIVE-TYPE CONFIGURATION IS:
                    Drive 1 is NOT ATTACHED
                    Drive 2 is NOT ATTACHED

                    HELP AVAILABLE BY PRESSING F1.

Unable to RESET the disk subsystem.

How many drives are attached to the AT compatible controller card? (Ø-2): 1
```

Figure 7.3: Modifying the CMOS configuration

```
HARD DISK MANAGEMENT PROGRAM  V3.3Ø    Drive  ,      Cyls by     heads.

                    CMOS CONFIGURATION UTILITY

              CURRENT CMOS DRIVE-TYPE CONFIGURATION IS:
                    Drive 1 is NOT ATTACHED
                    Drive 2 is NOT ATTACHED


Enter MODEL CODE for drive 1 (1-16, or RETURN if standard):

INSTALLING A STANDARD DRIVE.
Enter the DRIVE-TYPE-CODE, as recommended by the manufacturer of the computer
(as normally used during the manufacturer's drive installation process): 2
```

Figure 7.4: Specifying the hard disk type

The MFM hard disk drive has a storage capacity of 20 megabytes. It is equipped with 4 read-write heads and has 61 cylinders. With the BASIC program described in Step 5, the
number 2 was given as the hard disk type. At the DRIVE-
TYPE-CODE prompt, answer with the hard disk type given
by the BASIC program.

Now that your hard disk type is established, the new configuration will be entered into the computer's CMOS RAM.

In order for the computer to recognize the new configuration,
you have to reboot your computer. The DISK MANAGER

program will ask you to do this. Reboot from a floppy disk—
your hard disk is still not usable at this point.

When the computer displays the system prompt again, enter

   dm /m

to start DISK MANAGER again. The program will display its
main menu, as in Figure 7.5. Now you will initialize your
disk. Press I to select the Initialization option from the menu.
This brings up the Initialization menu, which is shown in Figure 7.6.

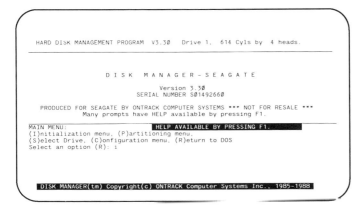

Figure 7.5: The DISK MANAGER main menu

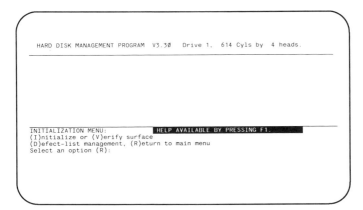

Figure 7.6: The Initialization menu

Before the program can initialize your disk, it must know where the bad tracks are. Press D to select the Defect-list management option from the Initialization menu.

Press A to select the Add to option and enter the hard disk errors listed on the error map. After you've entered each error, the program will ask you whether there are more errors to enter. Select the Add more to the Defect-List? option to enter more bad track numbers.

After you've reported all errors, you will be returned to the Initialization menu. The menu will now display a list of bad cylinders, as in Figure 7.7. This time press I to select the Initialize surface option. The program asks whether the listed hard disk errors are correct. Press Y for yes.

```
HARD DISK MANAGEMENT PROGRAM  V3.30    Drive 1,   614 Cyls by  4 heads.
─────────────────────────────────────────────────────────────────────
Cyl--Hd   Cyl--Hd   Cyl--Hd   Cyl--Hd   Cyl--Hd   Cyl--Hd   Cyl--Hd   Cyl--Hd
375- 2    609- 0




─────────────────────────── CURRENT DEFECT LIST ───────────────────────
INITIALIZATION MENU:
(I)nitialize or (V)erify surface
(D)efect-list management, (R)eturn to main menu
Select an option (R): i
Is the above DEFECT-LIST accurate for this disk? (y/n): y
Do a (T)rack, (P)artition, entire (D)isk,  (R)eturn to initialization menu
Select an option (R): d
Enter Interleave Value ( 3):
THIS WILL DESTROY ANY EXISTING DATA ON THIS DISK! CONTINUE ? (y/n):
```

Figure 7.7: Initializing a hard disk

Now you must initialize the entire hard disk—the tracks, partitions, etc. Answer the Do a Track, Partition, entire Disk, and Return to initialization menu prompts by pressing d, for disk.

One task remains to be done before the hard disk can be initialized: you can establish the interleave at the Enter Interleave Value prompt. A default value will already be displayed, but you can enter a default value of your own. With ATs, an interleave value of 3 is a good choice, and with fast computers 2 is sensible.

Now the hard disk is initialized. DISK MANAGER displays the following prompt:

```
THIS WILL DESTROY ANY EXISTING DATA ON
THIS DISK!
CONTINUE ? (y/n)
```

Press Y for yes.

Speedstor

Storage Dimensions offers another program for initializing hard disks called SpeedStor. Like DISK MANAGER, Speed-Stor contains various program modules and it can be installed automatically. Install the program automatically, if at all, only with hard disks that have a storage capacity larger than 32 megabytes and a DOS version prior to 3.3. Otherwise, install the program manually.

Since all DOS versions from 3.3 on can handle large partitions, an additional device driver such as the one SpeedStor installs is not required. Because SpeedStor is also compatible with RLL and ESDI hard disks, the program is shipped by many manufacturers along with their hard disks.

To initialize the hard disk, you need only the HARDPREP (prepare hard disk) program. This program comes on the SpeedStor disk.

To load the program, log onto the A drive and enter

```
hardprep
```

With RLL or ESDI controllers, you can also specify the number of sectors per track as a parameter. For example, the command for a hard disk with 35 sectors per track would be

```
hardprep /secs:35
```

After you've started the SpeedStor program, you see the screen shown in Figure 7.8.

```
SpeedStor(TM)  Hard Disk Preparation/Diagnostics, version 5.11
Copyright 1985,1988 Storage Dimensions, Inc.  (Special Micropolis version)
                        M A I N    M E N U
NextDrive  ComposeBTT  Diagnostics  Initialize  Type  ParkHeads  Quit

Select/Change Drive Specifications

Drive    Manufacturer/Model    Cyls  Heads  Secs  Precomp  Lzone  TotalBytes
  1           <no drive>         Ø     Ø     Ø     none     ?          Ø




                    To select a menu item:
    Use the arrow keys to highlight the desired option and press <Enter>,
            or type the first letter of the desired option.

            Press <Esc> to abort the current command.
        From the Main Menu, <Esc> will exit the program.
```

Figure 7.8: The SpeedStor main menu

The hard disk in the discussion that follows has a capacity of
20 megabytes. It has 615 cylinders and 4 read-write heads.
The park cylinder is found on cylinder 615. Each track should
be divided into 17 sectors.

Once again the hard disk should be initialized with an interleave of 3. However, the appropriate hard disk type has not
yet been determined. A partitioning should not be performed
until later with the DOS FDISK utility program.

Select the Type option from the main menu to bring up the
Drive Type menu, as shown in Figure 7.9. From here you

```
SpeedStor(TM)  Hard Disk Preparation/Diagnostics, version 5.11
Copyright 1985,1988 Storage Dimensions, Inc.  (Special Micropolis version)
                    D R I V E    T Y P E    M E N U
Quit  (1)DriveOne  (2)DriveTwo

Change Type of drive ONE (first drive)

Drive    Manufacturer/Model    Cyls  Heads  Secs  Precomp  Lzone  TotalBytes
  1           <no drive>         Ø     Ø     Ø     none     ?          Ø
```

Figure 7.9: The Drive Type menu

specify the hard disk type you're using. The sample screen was taken from SpeedStor software shipped with a Micropolis hard disk. You can select the correct Micropolis type designation without knowing the correct type number.

Since the hard disk in the sample screen was not manufactured by Micropolis, you specify the Standard-Type option. You'll see the screen in Figure 7.10.

```
SpeedStor(TM)  Hard Disk Preparation/Diagnostics, version 5.11
Copyright 1985,1988 Storage Dimensions, Inc.  (Special Micropolis version)

            Current Boot Type for drive 1 is (0). Over-ride type is (-1)

            Use cursor keys and press <Enter> to select the new drive type.
            IF you do not want to change the type, press ESC.

Drive    Manufacturer/Model     Cyls  Heads  Secs  Precomp  Lzone  TotalBytes
  1          <no drive>           0     0      0     none     ?          0
            S E L E C T   S T A N D A R D   R O M   T Y P E
Type  Cylinders  Heads  Sectors  PreComp  LandingZone  Ctrl   TotalBytes

<Standard Type, Manual Entry>
  1      306        4      17      128       305       0     10.653.696
  2      615        4      17      300       615       0     21.411.840
  3      615        6      17      300       615       0     32.117.760
  4      940        8      17      512       940       0     65.454.080
  5      940        6      17      512       940       0     49.090.560
  6      615        4      17      none      615       0     21.411.840
  7      462        8      17      256       511       0     32.169.984
  8      733        5      17      none      733       0     31.900.160
  9      900       15      17      none      901       0    117.504.000
                        Home  PgDn   ↑ ↓   PgUp  End
```

Figure 7.10: Choosing the connected hard disk

Next use the cursor movement keys to move the highlight bar to the standard type with the correct physical data. In Figure 7.10, this is type 6. Once you've selected the standard type, press enter.

This brings you back to the main menu again. Select the ComposeBTT option in order to enter hard disk errors from the bad track map. You'll see the Compose Bad Track Table menu, as shown in Figure 7.11.

Enter the errors with the Add command, as shown in Figure 7.12. Each time you will be prompted to give the Head number that corresponds to the appropriate side of the disk, as well as the corresponding cylinder. After you have entered all the errors, you can leave the menu by selecting Quit. When you're done, you'll be returned to the main menu.

Reporting errors

```
SpeedStor(TM)  Hard Disk Preparation/Diagnostics, version 5.11
Copyright 1985,1988 Storage Dimensions, Inc. (Special Micropolis version)

                  C O M P O S E   B A D   T R A C K   T A B L E
  Add  Revise  Delete  ScanSurface  ClearAll  Quit

  Add Another Track to Bad-Track Table

  Drive    Manufacturer/Model    Cyls  Heads  Secs  Precomp  Lzone  TotalBytes
    1      <Standard Type 2>     615     4     17     300     615   21.411.328




                        To select a menu item:
         Use the arrow keys to highlight the desired option and press <Enter>,
               or type the first letter of the desired option.

                     Press <Esc> to abort the current command.
               From the Main Menu, <Esc> will exit the program.
```

Figure 7.11: The Compose Bad Track Table menu

```
SpeedStor(TM)  Hard Disk Preparation/Diagnostics, version 5.11
Copyright 1985,1988 Storage Dimensions, Inc. (Special Micropolis version)

                    A D D   B A D   T R A C K   T O   T A B L E

  Enter Head Number of Bad Track: <0-3>        [    2]
  Enter Cylinder Number of Bad Track: <0-614>  [375  ]

  Drive    Manufacturer/Model    Cyls  Heads  Secs  Precomp  Lzone  TotalBytes
    1      <Standard Type 2>     615     4     17     300     615   21.411.328
      Page  1  of  1       B A D   T R A C K   T A B L E            1-Entries
  Head  Cyl    Head  Cyl    Head  Cyl    Head  Cyl    Head  Cyl    Head  Cyl
  ____  ___    ____  ___    ____  ___    ____  ___    ____  ___    ____  ___

   0    609
```

Figure 7.12: Designating the bad tracks

Specify interleave

Now you must inform the program of the interleave you want. Select Initialize to bring up the Initialization menu, as shown in Figure 7.13. Next, select the Interleave option and enter an interleave factor.

For instance, in the sample screen shown in Figure 7.14, an interleave factor of 3 has been selected. After you've selected the interleave factor you will return to the Initialization menu.

Notice the ReInitialize option. This option allows you to initialize the hard disk again and establish a new interleave without losing the data on the hard disk.

```
Speedstor(TM)  Hard Disk Preparation/Diagnostics, version 5.11
Copyright 1985,1988 Storage Dimensions, Inc. (Special Micropolis version)

                    I N I T I A L I Z A T I O N   M E N U

Quit  StandardInit  LockTracks  POD-fix  BoundedInit  ReInitialize

Perform 'Standard' Low Level Initialization

Drive    Manufacturer/Model     Cyls  Heads  Secs  Precomp  Lzone  TotalBytes
  1        <Standard Type 2>     615     4     17     3ØØ     615   21.411.328
   Page  1  of  1       B A D   T R A C K   T A B L E               2-Entries
  Head  Cyl     Head  Cyl    Head  Cyl    Head  Cyl    Head  Cyl    Head  Cyl

    Ø    6Ø9
    2    375
```

Figure 7.13: The Initialization menu

```
Speedstor(TM)  Hard Disk Preparation/Diagnostics, version 5.11
Copyright 1985,1988 Storage Dimensions, Inc. (Special Micropolis version)
                    I N I T I A L I Z E   D R I V E
                 The Default sector-INTERLEAVE factor is (3).
                 Enter the interleave factor <1-16> or
                 Press <Enter> to use the Default.    [  3]

Drive    Manufacturer/Model     Cyls  Heads  Secs  Precomp  Lzone  TotalBytes
  1        <Standard Type 2>     615     4     17     3ØØ     615   21.411.328
   Page  1  of  1       B A D   T R A C K   T A B L E               2-Entries
  Head  Cyl     Head  Cyl    Head  Cyl    Head  Cyl    Head  Cyl    Head  Cyl

    Ø    6Ø9
    2    375
```

Figure 7.14: Selecting an interleave factor

Now it's time to initialize your hard disk. Select the Standard Init option.

Standard Init

If you have any data on your hard disk, it will be erased during the next step. The program displays a warning message to this effect, as shown in Figure 7.15.

Verification question

Now select Initialize to begin initializing the hard disk, as in Figure 7.16.

```
SpeedStor(TM)  Hard Disk Preparation/Diagnostics, version 5.11
Copyright 1985,1988 Storage Dimensions, Inc.  (Special Micropolis version)
─────────────────────────────────────────────────────────────────────────
                    I N I T I A L I Z E    D R I V E
                  * * *    W A R N I N G    * * *
         This Function Will Destroy Data on Drive 1.
         Do you wish to proceed with the initialization?  No  Yes

Drive    Manufacturer/Model        Cyls  Heads  Secs  Precomp  Lzone  TotalBytes
  1        <Standard Type 2>        615     4     17     300     615   21.411.328
     Page  1  of  1     B A D    T R A C K    T A B L E              2-Entries
Head  Cyl      Head  Cyl      Head  Cyl      Head  Cyl      Head  Cyl      Head  Cyl
────          ────          ────          ────          ────          ────
  0   609
  2   375
```

Figure 7.15: Verifying initialization

```
SpeedStor(TM)  Hard Disk Preparation/Diagnostics, version 5.11
Copyright 1985,1988 Storage Dimensions, Inc.  (Special Micropolis version)
─────────────────────────────────────────────────────────────────────────
                    I N I T I A L I Z E    D R I V E

         Select 'Initialize' to start the low level format.  Quit  Initialize

Drive    Manufacturer/Model        Cyls  Heads  Secs  Precomp  Lzone  TotalBytes
  1        <Standard Type 2>        615     4     17     300     615   21.411.328
     Page  1  of  1     B A D    T R A C K    T A B L E              2-Entries
Head  Cyl      Head  Cyl      Head  Cyl      Head  Cyl      Head  Cyl      Head  Cyl
────          ────          ────          ────          ────          ────
  0   609
  2   375
```

Figure 7.16: Last verification before initialization

During initialization, the screen will display the cylinder that
is being operated on at that time, as in Figure 7.17.

When the initialization is finished, you will see a screen like
the one in Figure 7.18. You can press any key to return to the
Initialization menu. From there you can return to the main
menu by selecting Quit. To return to DOS, select Quit again.

```
SpeedStor(TM)  Hard Disk Preparation/Diagnostics, version 5.11
Copyright 1985,1988 Storage Dimensions, Inc.  (Special Micropolis version)
                    I N I T I A L I Z E   D R I V E
                    INITIALIZING DRIVE, PLEASE WAIT

                    Heads 0-3  Cylinder  613

Drive    Manufacturer/Model      Cyls  Heads  Secs  Precomp  Lzone  TotalBytes
  1        <Standard Type 2>      615     4     17     300     615   21.411.328
   Page  1  of  1      B A D   T R A C K   T A B L E             2-Entries
Head  Cyl      Head  Cyl    Head  Cyl    Head  Cyl    Head  Cyl    Head  Cyl

  0    609
  2    375
```

Figure 7.17: Beginning of the initialization

```
SpeedStor(TM)  Hard Disk Preparation/Diagnostics, version 5.11
Copyright 1985,1988 Storage Dimensions, Inc.  (Special Micropolis version)



HardPrep is Done

A>
```

Figure 7.18: The initialization procedure is finished.

After the hard disk has been initialized, you can reassemble
the computer chassis. But first turn the power off and pull the
plug from the socket. Removing the additional connection
cables (keyboard, monitor, printer) gives you more freedom of
movement when the times come to put the computer back
together.

The Partition Table

The partition table tells which area of the hard disk is designated to which operating system. Partitioning allows you to load four different operating systems on one computer and one hard disk. With diskettes, there is no such physical division of storage media.

Each operating system, whether DOS, OS/2, or UNIX, is given its own partition on the hard disk. As a rule, each operating system can only access its own partition. For example, DOS can only access portions reserved for DOS, and UNIX can only access the corresponding UNIX area. There is an exception to this rule, however. Because DOS and OS/2 have the same disk format, they can access one another's partitions. The partition table for each partition contains instructions regarding its beginning, end, and length. So that the computer will know which operating system should be loaded when booting up, one of the four partitions can be set to "active" status.

To make a partition active, use the DOS FDISK utility program. This way, the next time you turn on your computer it will automatically load the operating system on the partition you selected. The FDISK program comes with DOS. Besides using it to make a partition active, you can create a DOS partition with the FDISK program. This is discussed below.

FDISK

Until DOS Version 3.3, the maximum size of a DOS partition was limited to 32 megabytes. But starting with Version 3.3, larger partitions became possible. A larger partition can still be divided into several logical drives. Each logical drive can have a maximum size of 32 megabytes. The reason 32 megabytes is the maximum size has to do with the structure of the file allocation table (FAT). Because DOS Version 3.3 uses a 16-bit FAT, each partition can be divided into a maximum of $2^{16}=65536$ sectors for every 512 bytes—that is, 32 megabytes.

With DOS 4.0, it became possible to create a 32-bit FAT. Because of its size, however, a partition with a 32-bit FAT is inaccessible to earlier versions of DOS. Furthermore, a 32-bit FAT creates difficulties for many hard-disk-oriented utility programs. On the other hand, a partition with 32-bit FAT is no longer limited to 32 megabytes.

The Boot Record

Information about the four possible partitions is stored in the first sector on the first track of the first head. This sector is called the boot record.

The partition table is part of the boot record. Besides the partition table, some error messages are stored in the boot record, as are exact specifications about how DOS should manage the hard disk. The names of the system files—IBMBIO.COM and IBMDOS.COM or IO.SYS and MSDOS.SYS—are also in the boot record. There is a small program in the boot record for loading and executing system files as well.

Clusters

Each file, depending on how many bytes it takes up, is stored on a certain number of sectors. These sectors are combined to form clusters. A file that contains only 10 bytes requires the same amount of space as a file that contains 2000 bytes—both are stored in one cluster. The point is, the smallest storage unit on which a file can be stored is a cluster, not a sector.

How big a cluster is depends on the DOS version being used and the capacity of the hard disk. For example, on a hard disk with a capacity of 70 megabytes, 8 sectors make a cluster.

The name of a file is entered in the directory on which it was created, and so is the number of the first cluster occupied by the file. Information about the other clusters that store the file is found in the FAT.

File Allocation Table (FAT)

Each cluster on the hard disk is allocated a specific bit in the file allocation table.Defective sectors are also recorded in the FAT. So that DOS can access cluster information very quickly while you are operating the computer, a copy of the FAT is retained in main memory.

Step 9:

DOS Version 3.2x

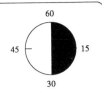

Installing DOS through Version 3.2x

Place the working copy of your system diskette in drive A and turn on the power switch to your computer. The computer will boot the operating system from the diskette in drive A. After the boot procedure is completed, the computer signifies that it is ready by displaying either of two DOS prompts:

    A>

or

    A:\>

Before the operating system can be copied onto the hard disk, you must create a DOS partition. A DOS partition establishes the area that later will be available to you for your work under DOS. The area can take up a maximum of 32 megabytes on your hard disk. Only one DOS partition is allowed. This is a limitation of all DOS versions up to and including DOS 3.2x, but beginning with version 3.3, hard disks with higher capacities can be managed using several DOS partitions.

Creating a DOS partition

The DISK MANAGER and SpeedStor programs, which are discussed in Step 7, let you use hard disks with a capacity of more than 32 megabytes with DOS versions prior to 3.3.

With DISK MANAGER and SpeedStor, several DOS partitions can be addressed using device drivers.

FDISK

Type FDISK at the DOS prompt and press return. The DOS program for partitioning the hard disk is loaded from the system diskette in drive A into memory. If you are using IBM PC-DOS version 3.20, your screen will look like Figure 9.1. With other DOS versions, the screen may differ slightly.

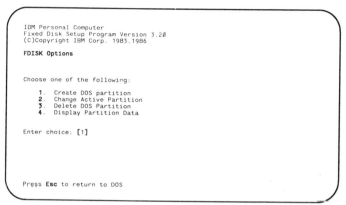

```
IBM Personal Computer
Fixed Disk Setup Program Version 3.20
(C)Copyright IBM Corp. 1983,1986

FDISK Options


Choose one of the following:

    1.  Create DOS partition
    2.  Change Active Partition
    3.  Delete DOS Partition
    4.  Display Partition Data

Enter choice: [1]



Press Esc to return to DOS
```

Figure 9.1: The FDISK 3.20 main menu

Select option 1, Create DOS partition, by pressing return. Your screen should look like the one in Figure 9.2. Now you can specify how large your DOS partition should be.

```
Create DOS Partition


Do you wish to use the entire fixed
disk for DOS (Y/N)............? [Y]







Press Esc to return to FDISK Options
```

Figure 9.2: Creating a DOS partition

 Menu option 5, Select next hard disk, appears only when two hard disks are present.

Press the return key to accept the default value and produce the largest possible DOS partition. Your screen should look like Figure 9.3. The DOS partition you choose will simultaneously be selected as the active one. Next time you boot the computer, as long as there is no diskette in drive A, the operating system will be loaded from the hard disk.

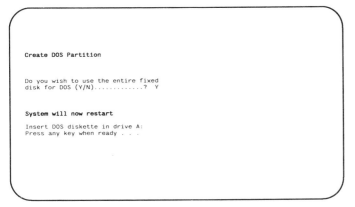

```
Create DOS Partition

Do you wish to use the entire fixed
disk for DOS (Y/N).............?  Y

System will now restart

Insert DOS diskette in drive A:
Press any key when ready . . .
```

Figure 9.3: Establishing the partition size

Leave the system diskette in drive A and press return again. The computer will reboot. After the system is loaded into memory again from the diskette, it will acknowledge the new DOS partition.

However, the newly created DOS partition must be formatted before it can work. In order to format the DOS partition, issue the DOS FORMAT command. Enter

        FORMAT C:/S

C is the drive letter designation for the first hard disk. /S copies the command line interpreter (COMMAND.COM) and the two DOS hidden files (IBMBIO.COM and IBMDOS.COM) onto the hard disk after the hard disk formatting procedure of the disk operating system (DOS).

DOS partition formatting

Now the operating system can be loaded from the hard disk during the boot procedure. But before you reboot your computer again, the remaining files of your operating system have to be copied to your hard disk.

Creating CONFIG.-SYS and AUTO-EXEC.BAT

You will create two additional files, CONFIG.SYS and AUTOEXEC.BAT, and a subdirectory called DOS. To create these, follow the procedures below:

```
A>C:

C>MD DOS

C>A:

A>C:

C>CD ..

C>COPY CON CONFIG.SYS
BUFFERS=20
FILES=20
^Z

1 file(s) copied

C>COPY CON AUTOEXEC.BAT
PATH=C:\DOS;C:\;
PROMPT $P$G
VER
^Z

1 file(s) copied
```

Now that you've finished installing DOS, remove the diskette from drive A and reboot your computer again by pressing Ctrl, Alt, and Del all at once.

Done!

The computer loads the operating system from the hard disk.

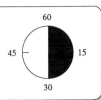

Step 10:

DOS Version 3.3

Installing DOS 3.3

Place a working copy of your DOS 3.3 startup disk in drive A and boot the computer by turning on the power switch. After the boot procedure is completed, the computer will display either of two DOS prompts: A> or A:\>.

Each DOS version, version 3.3 included, requires you to create a DOS partition with the DOS FDISK command. The partition establishes the area that will be available to you for later work with DOS. Under DOS 3.3, two types of partitions can be created, primary partitions and extended partitions.

Create a partition with FDISK

Before you can create an extended partition, you must create a primary partition. You must do this because the operating system is loaded from the primary partition.

A primary partition has a maximum size of 32 megabytes, and an extended partition can take up the remaining storage space on the hard disk. The extended partition can hold several logical drives, each of which can have a maximum of 32 megabytes.

Partitioning a hard disk under DOS 3.3 is as simple as partitioning a hard disk with earlier DOS versions. In fact, all you have to do in most cases is press return to accept the defaults. The defaults are correctly given by the program.

This step shows you how to partition a typical hard disk with a primary partition and several logical drives in the extended DOS partition. (The hard disk in the example has a storage capacity of 71 megabytes.)

Additional device drivers are not required.

At the DOS prompt, type FDISK. The DOS program for partitioning the hard disk will be loaded from the diskette in drive A into memory. Your screen should look like Figure 10.1.

To create a DOS partition, just press return. By doing this you select Option 1, Create DOS Partition. Now your screen will look like Figure 10.2.

Since you are going to create a primary DOS partition, press return again to select option 1, Create Primary DOS partition. You will see the screen in Figure 10.3.

```
IBM Personal Computer
Fixed Disk Setup Program Version 3.30
(C)Copyright IBM Corp. 1983,1987

FDISK Options

Current Fixed Disk Drive: 1

Choose one of the following:

     1. Create DOS partition
     2. Change Active Partition
     3. Delete DOS partition
     4. Display Partition Information



Enter choice: [1]



Press ESC to return to DOS
```

Figure 10.1: The DOS FDISK 3.3 main menu

```
Create DOS Partition

Current Fixed Disk Drive: 1


     1. Create Primary DOS partition
     2. Create Extended DOS partition



Enter choice: [1]



Press ESC to return to FDISK Options
```

Figure 10.2: Creating a DOS partition

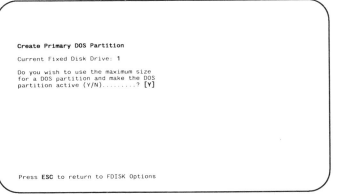

```
Create Primary DOS Partition

Current Fixed Disk Drive: 1

Do you wish to use the maximum size
for a DOS partition and make the DOS
partition active (Y/N).........? [Y]




Press ESC to return to FDISK Options
```

Figure 10.3: Creating a primary DOS partition

Press return again to generate the largest possible primary partition. By pressing return, you also make the primary partition active at the same time. That is, the next time you start your computer—as long as there is no diskette in drive A—the operating system will be loaded from the hard disk. Your screen should look like Figure 10.4. Leave the system diskette in drive A and press return again. The system now reboots.

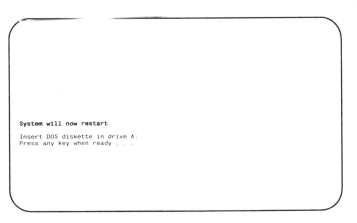

```
System will now restart

Insert DOS diskette in drive A:
Press any key when ready . . .
```

Figure 10.4: Reboot request

Now that the operating system is loaded from the diskette, it acknowledges the primary partition. If your hard disk has a maximum capacity of more than 32 megabytes, you must also create an extended DOS partition. To do this you use the FDISK command again. Type FDISK at the DOS prompt. Your screen will look like Figure 10.5.

To create an extended partition from the main menu, press return once to select the Create DOS partition option. Your screen will look like Figure 10.6.

Creating an extended DOS partition

Because you want to create an extended DOS partition this time, press the 2 key, and then press return. Your screen will look like Figure 10.7.

```
IBM Personal Computer
Fixed Disk Setup Program Version 3.30
(C)Copyright IBM Corp. 1983,1987

FDISK Options

Current Fixed Disk Drive: 1

Choose one of the following:

     1. Create DOS partition
     2. Change Active Partition
     3. Delete DOS partition
     4. Display Partition Information


Enter choice: [1]



Press ESC to return to DOS
```

Figure 10.5: The DOS FDISK main menu called up again

```
Create DOS Partition

Current Fixed Disk Drive: 1


     1. Create Primary DOS partition
     2. Create Extended DOS partition



Enter choice: [2]



Press ESC to return to FDISK Options
```

Figure 10.6: Establishing of a DOS partition for the remaining area of the hard disk

Press return to select the default and organize the remaining space on the hard disk into an extended DOS partition, as in Figure 10.8.

Next, follow the directions of the program. Press Esc (the escape key is usually on the corner of the numeric keypad) to back out of the menu and press return to produce a logical drive with the maximum size of 32 megabytes, as in Figure 10.9. Since the extended DOS partition has yet to be assigned a logical drive, the program prompts you to specify a size for the logical drive, as in Figure 10.10.

Press return one more time to accept the default and organize the remaining area of the extended DOS partition into an

```
Create Extended DOS Partition

Current Fixed Disk Drive: 1

Partition Status   Type  Start  End Size
  C: 1          A   PRI DOS    0  480  481


Total disk space is 1023 cylinders.
Maximum space available for partition
is  542 cylinders.
Enter partition size...........: [ 542]



Press ESC to return to FDISK Options
```

Figure 10.7: Creating an extended DOS partition

```
Create Extended DOS Partition

Current Fixed Disk Drive: 1

Partition Status   Type  Start  End Size
  C: 1          A   PRI DOS    0  480  481
     2              EXT DOS  481 1022  542




Extended DOS partition created

Press ESC to return to FDISK Options
```

Figure 10.8: Establishing the size of the extended partition

```
Create Logical DOS Drive(s)




No logical drives defined


Total partition size is  542 cylinders.
Maximum space available for logical
drive is  481 cylinders.
Enter logical drive size........: [ 481]


Press ESC to return to FDISK Options
```

Figure 10.9: Establishing the partition size

```
Create Logical DOS Drive(s)

Drv Start End  Size
 D:  481  961  481




Total partition size is  542 cylinders.
Maximum space available for logical
drive is  61 cylinders.
Enter logical drive size........: [  61]
Logical DOS drive created, drive letters
changed or added
Press ESC to return to FDISK Options
```

Figure 10.10: Establishing the first logical drive

additional logical drive, as in Figure 10.11.

You must also reboot the computer. Your screen should look like Figure 10.12. Now press Esc twice to make the computer reboot again.

The DOS partitions and logical drives you just created must still be formatted. To do this, issue the DOS FORMAT command. Enter

```
FORMAT C:/S
```

at the DOS prompt. C is the drive letter for the first hard disk and the /S copies the command line interpreter

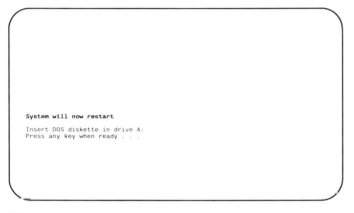

```
Create Logical DOS Drive(s)

Drv Start End  Size
 D:   481   961  481
 E:   962  1022   61




All available space in the Extended DOS
partition is assigned to logical drives.

Logical DOS drive created, drive letters
changed or added
Press ESC to return to FDISK Options
```

Figure 10.11: Establishing an additional disk drive

```
System will now restart

Insert DOS diskette in drive A:
Press any key when ready . . .
```

Figure 10.12: Reboot request

(COMMAND.COM) onto the hard disk after the formatting procedure of the disk operating system. (DOS stands for Disk Operating System.)

To format the logical drives, in this example D and E, use the FORMAT command again, this time without additional parameters. Just enter

    FORMAT D:

and

    FORMAT E:

Press return after each entry.

Step 9 explains how to copy all the remaining files of your system diskette. As before, you will create two files, CONFIG.SYS and AUTOEXEC.BAT, and a directory called DOS. To do this, simply repeat the following printed dialog at this point with your computer.

```
A>c:

C>md dos

C>cd dos

A>copy a:*.* c:

C>cd ..

C>copy con config.sys
buffers=20
files=20
^Z          1 file(s) copied

C>copy con autoexec.bat
path=c:\dos; c:\;
prompt $p$G
ver
^Z          1 file(s) copied
```

Remove the diskette from drive A. Reboot your computer now by simultaneously pressing Ctrl, Alt, and Del.

The computer loads the operating system from the hard disk.

Step 11:

DOS Version 4.0

Installing DOS 4.0

Installing DOS version 4.0 is quite simple. Besides the diskettes that come with DOS 4.0, you need one blank diskette to
install the program. During the installation procedure, you'll
need the following diskettes:

> DOS 4.0 INSTALL
> DOS 4.0 SELECT
> DOS 4.0 OPERATING1
> DOS 4.0 OPERATING2
> DOS 4.0 OPERATING3
> DOS 4.0 SHELL (in case you want to install the DOS
> user shell)
> a blank diskette (labeled "SELECT COPY")

The program will prompt you to insert each of these diskettes.

To install DOS version 4.0, follow the instructions below.

Insert the INSTALL diskette in drive A and start the computer.
The computer will boot from the diskette in drive A.

Follow the instructions of the DOS 4.0 installation program.
Remove the INSTALL diskette from drive A and insert the
SELECT diskette in its place.

The opening screen informs you that you need a blank diskette during the installation procedure.

The program will display a series of selection menus. As you
work through these menus, remember that you can reach the
next one by pressing return, or press Esc to go back to the previous menu. Use the cursor movement keys (→, ←, ↑ and ↓)

to select the various options on the menus. Make your menu choice by pressing return. If you have any questions about the procedures, press F1 to activate the Help function. The rest of this step deals with the important questions the program will ask—the other questions are self-explanatory.

Installation onto the Hard Disk

The DOS 4.0 operating system is installed on the hard disk, so select C: when the program prompts you where DOS is installed. When the program asks into which subdirectory the operating system should be copied, press return. By doing this, you create a default subdirectory called DOS on the hard disk. Later, the utility programs of the operating system will be copied into this subdirectory.

Printer Selection

One of the selection menus will ask you how many printers are connected to your system. If you have no printers attached, answer 0 to this question.

Selecting printers

But if you do have one or more printers connected, the program will display a list of printers for you to select. If your printer is not on the list, select the printer that comes the closest to its driver sequences. This is often the IBM 5152 Graphics Printer Model 2 or the IBM 4201 Proprinter. As a rule, the proper printer port carries the designation LPT1.

DOS User Shell

Further along in the installation procedure you will be asked whether you want to install the DOS shell. The DOS shell program, an interface that lets you issue DOS commands from menus instead of with keyboard commands, is easy to use and especially helpful for beginners.

You will be asked to verify that you have finished responding to the prompts, and then you will be asked to insert various diskettes that come with the program.

Before the installation procedure begins, a working diskette is created by the installation program. Label this diskette "SELECT COPY."

Next follows the partitioning of the hard disk. Before the installation program will acknowledge a new partitioning, you have to reboot your computer. Do this by pressing Ctrl, Alt, and Del all at once.

The hard disk is formatted and the operating system is copied onto the hard disk. At this point you will be prompted to insert the OPERATING 1, 2, and 3 diskettes into the floppy drive.

As soon as the installation procedure is successfully concluded, you will be requested to reboot the computer once more.

You have just completed the menu-driven installation procedure for DOS 4.0. Now the DOS operating system is on your hard disk.

Very easy
for
beginners
to install

Besides a menu-driven installation, a manual installation is also possible in version 4.0. The manual installation procedure is the same as that described for DOS 3.3 in Step 10. Still, in order to rule out possible errors you should use menu-driven installation.

Step 12:

OS/2 Installation

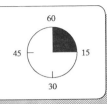

Installing OS/2 is just as easy as installing DOS 4.0. The only difference is that OS/2 requires an 80286 or 80386 processor. OS/2 can't be installed on an XT. Furthermore, Microsoft recommends having at least 2 megabytes of memory for OS/2.

A hard disk with a storage capacity of at least 40 megabytes and a fast access time gives the OS/2 system additional speed advantages when it accesses the hard disk.

Insert the diskette labeled INSTALL in drive A and start the computer. During the entire installation procedure you will be lead by a menu.

Don't forget to complete any of the steps. You will complete the following operations in sequence:

1. Creating an OS/2 partition on the hard disk.
2. Formatting the hard disk.
3. Creating the necessary OS/2 directories.
4. Copying the required files into their respective directories.

After the installation procedure is completed, you can start your computer from your hard disk.

Programs that can run under DOS without a hitch will not necessarily function under OS/2.

Step 13:

UNIX Installation

Unfortunately, it's hard to describe how to install UNIX in general terms because there are many different versions of the system. There are also many different variations on how it was "ported over." Consult the instructions that came with your UNIX operating system for help with the details.

As is the case with some DOS versions and also with OS/2, a specific section, or partition of the hard disk is placed at the disposal of the UNIX operating system by the installation procedure.

Pay particular attention to the differences between the various DOS versions, including OS/2, and UNIX. UNIX programs are just as unlikely to run under DOS or OS/2 as DOS or OS/2 programs are to run under the UNIX operating system.

The reason for this lies in the fundamentally different construction of the UNIX operating system. In contrast to DOS, UNIX is a multiuser system. Nevertheless, utility programs are available that make it possible to load a DOS program from a DOS partition inside UNIX. With these programs you can even transport data from a DOS partition into UNIX. Ask your UNIX supplier about these programs.

Absolutely crucial for the installation of a UNIX system is a computer with an 80286, or better still an 80386, processor. A main memory of at least 1.5 megabytes is also required. Only then can UNIX provide proof of its suitability as a multiuser system.

At the very minimum, you need a hard disk with at least a 20-megabyte storage capacity to use UNIX. Just to install the operating system requires 10 megabytes. Once application programs are added to this, you quickly reach the limits of storage

At least a 20 megabyte hard disk

capacity if you have a 20-megabyte hard disk. You should have a hard disk with a capacity of at least 70 megabytes to run UNIX.

If you want to end a UNIX work session, execute the Shutdown command. This command has nothing in common with the program by the same name for parking hard disks. You should always issue this command before you turn your computer off. This command tells all connected users that the computer will be turned off in a few moments. Each connected user will have enough time to end the program he or she is in at that time.

Computer Systems with Two Hard Disks under DOS

Sequence

With computers that only have one hard disk drive, the scheme by which the various drive letter designations are assigned a partition is quite simple:

C: primary DOS partition
D: first logical drive of the extended DOS partition
E: first logical drive of the extended DOS partition,
   and so on

There also may be a RAM disk with its drive letter designation and another drive letter for a floppy drive.

The scheme by which two installed hard disks are assigned partitions is entirely different:

C: primary DOS partition of the first hard disk
D: primary DOS partition of the second hard disk

All the logical drives in the extended partition of the first hard disk follow, and afterwards come all the logical drives in the extended partition of the second hard disk. Next comes any RAM disk that may be present.

Division with Regard to Contents

In practice, dividing the two hard disks by contents is very sensible. For instance, you could place all DOS utility programs and other frequently needed utilities on drive C. Drive D would be used exclusively for a database. Of course, this applies in the same way to the logical drives of an extended DOS partition.

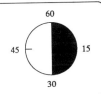

Step 15:

Data Backup

As time goes by a wealth of data accumulates on a hard disk, and backing up this data is important. Users should back up their data on diskettes or streamer tapes. When an important file is lost from the hard disk, you'll wish you had made a data backup of that file. Restoring a data file that has been backed up is a simple matter.

Probably the easiest way to backup data is to use the DOS BACKUP and RESTORE utility programs.

DOS utility programs

Take note, however, that a backup produced under one DOS version cannot be restored with the RESTORE command of another DOS version.

Apart from that, various software manufacturers offer diverse backup programs. Since the programs don't differ from each other in any essential way, we'll use the Back-It program from Gazelle Systems as an example of how to use a backup program.

The Back-It Program

Back-It is a flexible backup program. This program allows you to make backup copies of all mass-storage media that work under DOS. The backup itself is made onto diskettes. The program is not fussy about the diskettes to which the backup is copied. All diskette formats, whether 5.25-inch, 3.5-inch, 360-kilobyte, or even 1.44-megabyte, are readily accepted.

Even if a backup diskette turns out to have errors, the entire backup copy is not necessarily unusable. Back-It provides special error algorithms and correction mechanisms to help restore your data in just such a case.

The menu-driven program is easy to use. No matter what the current procedure you're trying to complete, you can call up additional help with the F1 key. A 360-kilobyte diskette is filled in 17 seconds with backup data. The corresponding time for a 1.2 megabyte diskette is only about 28 seconds.

Before you begin the backup procedure, Back-It lets you decide which files should be backed up and which ones should be left out of the backup. For example, you can back up all files with a given date or all files in a given subdirectory. Files already backed up during a previous backup procedure need not be backed up again. During the restore procedure, you need not restore all files; you may restore only one.

If the diskettes for the backup procedure have not been formatted, Back-It will format them automatically. The program is excellent in every respect.

Other programs for creating backup data are: FastBack and FastBack Plus from Fifth Generation Systems, Flashback from Overland Data (Shareware), Pdisk from Phoenix Technologies, and PC Tools Deluxe from Central Point Software.

Streamer Tape Backup

Another way to back up data is with streamer tape. This techique is gaining in popularity all the time because you don't have to constantly swap disks and the data backup takes significantly less time.

This backup method employs special tape-recorder-like devices called tape streamers or simply tape backups.

With most devices, the accompanying software offers two options for data backup: it can copy the entire contents of the hard disk, or individual files. Backing up the entire hard disk is called "image backup."

Backing up individual files is called "file backup." Depending on the number and the length of the files to be copied, both procedures have their advantages and disadvantages. The image backup of a hard disk can hold many long files and is considerably quicker than a file backup of the same hard disk.

On the other hand, if there are only a few short files on the hard disk, a file backup takes considerably less time.

Tape backup devices that include data backup programs are offered by Wangtek, Irwin, and Archive. The various systems differ, among other things, in the size of the tape cassette used and the recording procedure used. Current recording procedures for streamer tapes are QIC-11 and QIC-24.

Moreover, devices with their own driver cards must be differentiated from those that are connected along with the floppy drives to the disk controller. Devices connected to the disk controller transmit data at a considerably slower rate than the type with its own driver card.

If a computer chassis has no space available for installing a tape backup, you can use an external tape backup device. These are usually connected by way of a 25-pin cable to the driver card inside the computer.

The accompanying software usually doesn't leave much to be desired. Fully automated data backups represent no problems with these devices to a certain point.

Nevertheless, streamer tape backups have a significant disadvantage: they are not cheap. For a reasonable device you must pay nearly $1000. By far the most economical way to back up data is to use diskettes.

Step 16:

DOS Commands

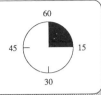

DOS Commands and Hard Disks

BUFFERS=20

Enter the BUFFERS=20 command in the CONFIG.SYS file. This command sets the buffers for the operating system. Buffers are storage areas that temporarily hold the data that is being transferred from one device to another. All write and read accesses of the hard disk pass over the buffers. If a request is made for the data on a certain sector in the hard disk and that data is already in a buffer, the data doesn't need to be loaded from the disk again. Establishing 20 buffers will suffice in most cases.

FILES=20

Enter the FILES=20 command in the CONFIG.SYS. Both the BUFFERS=20 and FILES=20 commands should be in the configuration file.

The FILES=20 command establishes the maximum number of files that the program can directly address at the same time.

PATH

You use the PATH command to inform the operating system that you want to call up a new program. Specifically, you tell the operating system in which drive and in which directory to search for the new program.

For example, suppose you were in a subdirectory called DATA on drive C and you wanted to format a diskette. To do this you need the FORMAT program, which is in the DOS directory, not the DATA subdirectory.

To format the diskette you could change to the DOS directory, call up the FORMAT program, and change back to the DATA directory. But there is a better, easier way. To spare yourself the work of having to change drives and directories, you could use a PATH command to state where the program should be looked for.

You can have the operating system look in several drives or subdirectories at once by linking several path statements. To link path statements, place a semicolon between each one, as in the example below.

```
C>path=c:\dos;c:\util;d:\max\tools;
```

This path statement tells the operating system to search in the current directory, and, if necessary, to search in the next directory to see if the program is located there. In the example, the operating system will look in the DOS and UTIL subdirectories on drive C, as well as the TOOLS subdirectory in the MAX subdirectory on drive C.

Avoid using long path statements—it is easy to enter one letter wrong when calling up a program.

If you enter one letter wrong in a path statement with ten subdirectories, for example, it will take a long time before the program will tell you that you made an error.

The PATH command works only for .EXE, .COM, and .BAT.

PROMPT

The PROMPT command lets you make a prompt of your own. You could even create a command prompt that says, "Your next command?"

Enter the PROMPT PG command and DOS will display a prompt that tells you on which drive and in which directory you are at the time. Figure 16.1 shows the results of different PROMPT commands.

```
C:\>prompt
C>cd dos
C>cd ..
C>prompt $p$g
C:\>cd dos
C:\DOS>cd ..
C:\>prompt Your next command: $_$p$g
Your next command:
C:\>
```

Figure 16.1: The PROMPT command

The PROMPT command syntax is as follows:

```
PROMPT character_string
```

Besides a prompt of your own design, you can use predefined character sequences to create a prompt. Predefined character sequences always begin with the dollar sign ($) prefix. For example, typing $d at the prompt will make the system display the current date. Table 16.1 shows the predefined character sequences and their functions.

Predefined characters

Character combination	Function
$$	Displays a dollar sign
$b	Displays the broken vertical character (¦)
$d	Displays the current date
$e	Presses the escape key (used for ANSI screen control sequences)
$g	Displays the greater than character (>)
$h	Presses a backspace

Table 16.1: Predefined Character Sequences for the PROMPT Command

Character combination	Function
$l	Displays the less than character (<)
$p	Displays the name of the current directory
$q	Displays the equal sign (=)
$t	Displays the current time
$v	Displays the version number of DOS
$_	Display the text that follow in the character string on the next line

Table 16.1: Predefined Character Sequences for the PROMPT Command (cont.)

SET

The SET command allows you to assign system variables such as COMSPEC, PATH, and PROMPT, just like individual variables. The syntax of the command is

```
SET variable_name=character_string
```

You can use the predefined system variables COMSPEC, PATH, and PROMPT, or your own variable names can be used. For example, the character string below assigns the name "Maexchen" to the given variable.

```
C>set name=maexchen
```

If the SET command is called up without any arguments, it shows the settings of the various variables, as in Figure 16.2.

VER

The VER command shows you which operating system version you have loaded. Many programs require you to use a specific DOS version.

For example, in order to find out if DOS version 3.3 is really on the hard disk you booted from, you would enter the VER command, and the version number of the operating system would be displayed immediately. Figure 16.3 shows the results of the VER command.

```
C:\>set
COMSPEC=C:\COMMAND.CO
PATH=C:\DOS;C:\;
BINKLEY=d:\mailbox
DSZPORT=4
OPALPORT=4
OPALTASK=Ø
PROMPT=$p$g

C:\>set name=max

C:\>set
COMSPEC=C:\COMMAND.COM
PATH=C:\DOS;C:\;
BINKLEY=d:\mailbox
DSZPORT=4
OPALPORT=4
OPALTASK=Ø
PROMPT=$p$g
NAME=max

C:\>
```

Figure 16.2: The SET command

```
C:\>ver

MS-DOS Version 3.3Ø

C:\>prompt $v$_$p$g

MS-DOS Version 3.3Ø
C:\>
```

Figure 16.3: The VER command

89

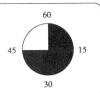

Utilities, Their Use and Benefits

PC Tools Deluxe

The PC Tools Deluxe software package contains various utilities for daily use. The PCSETUP program automatically installs software on your hard disk. And if you want, the AUTOEXEC.BAT file will be configured for PCTOOLS during the installation process.

Various utilities in PC Tools

The PC Tools software package contains several utilities that can be combined with the PCSHELL program for manipulating data and information about files and diskette contents.

The DIRECTORY command shows you the names of all directories and subdirectories. Accidentally erased files can be restored with the UNDELETE command.

The LOCATE and SEARCH commands look through a specific file on the hard disk. The COMPARE command compares two files or two diskettes to find out if they're identical.

With the PRINT command you can send a text file to the printer. The SYS INFO command gives you details about system information.

A single command, PCSHELL, gives you access to all of the aforementioned commands at once. Figure 17.1 shows the PC Tools opening screen.

A program for formatting diskettes called PCFORMAT is provided with the PC Tools Deluxe utility. The time required to format a diskette with this program is far less than the time required using the DOS FORMAT command.

PCFORMAT

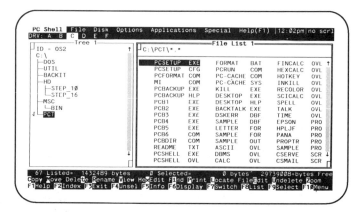

Figure 17.1: The PC Tools opening screen

PCFORMAT is called up in the same way that you call up the DOS FORMAT command. The PC Tools Deluxe installation program replaces the DOS command—that is, the program uses the PCSHELL program to display a user interface outfitted with windows and pull-down menus. Thanks to the interface, two directories can be displayed on the screen at the same time.

Simple usage

The PCTOOLS functions also appear on this user interface. There is also a screen-oriented editor and other functions. You will soon see that working with the user interface is noticeably simpler than working with the various DOS utility programs. You can get in-depth descriptions of the PC Tools commands at any time by pressing F1.

PCBACKUP

The PCBACKUP program offers a very convenient data backup feature. In order to reduce the number of diskettes you need to back up your data, you can compress the contents of the files before you write them onto backup diskettes. Individual files can be backed up, and so can entire directories. All sorts of criteria can be specified in a SETUP file. That way, during future backups, only the SETUP file has to be loaded. Figure 17.2 shows the opening screen of the PCBACKUP program.

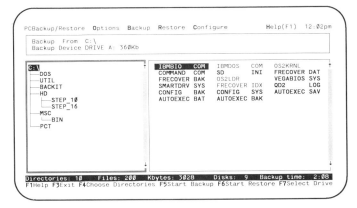

Figure 17.2: The PCBACKUP program

Various programs for daily use are included in the DESKTOP program. These programs can be seen in the main menu, which is shown in Figure 17.3.

DESKTOP

Choose the notepad option to activate the NOTEPAD command. The size of your note is limited by the program to 64,000 characters. This is no problem in practice, though, since the program handles several notepads. Each notepad is stored in a separate file. A sample notepad is shown in Figure 17.4.

Notepad

An Appointment Calendar for daily appointment planning is also provided. You can schedule a new appointment every

Appoint-
ment
calendar

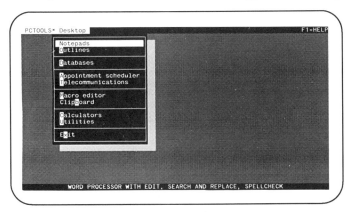

Figure 17.3: The DESKTOP main menu

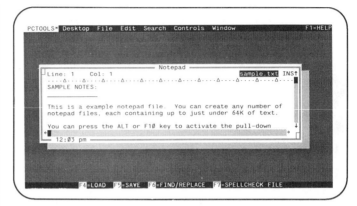

Figure 17.4: The Notepad

fifteen minutes. You can also schedule holidays and vacations. The menu for the Appointment Calendar is shown in Figure 17.5.

Database

You can set up a database with the DATABASE command, which is shown in Figure 17.6. The DATABASE command allows you to produce page layouts for the input and output of your data. Naturally, commands for sorting your records are also available to you. You can archive your records or photos with the DATABASE command. All data records can also be printed, of course.

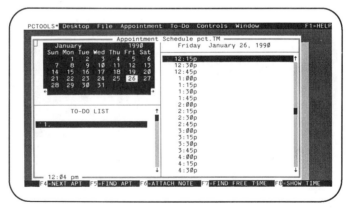

Figure 17.5: The Appointment Calendar

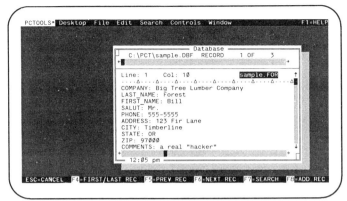

Figure 17.6: The DATABASE command

The CALCULATORS command lets you select from three calculators: a simple calculator, a business calculator that is comparable to the HP-12C from Hewlett-Packard, and a programmer's calculator that can handle hexadecimal, octal, binary, and decimal numbers.

Calculator

A communications program for the serial transmission of data is also available with the Telecommunications command. All important parameters of data transmission can be set. The opening screen of the Telecommunications command is shown in Figure 17.8.

User-friendly data transmission

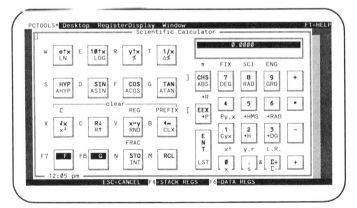

Figure 17.7: The Calculator

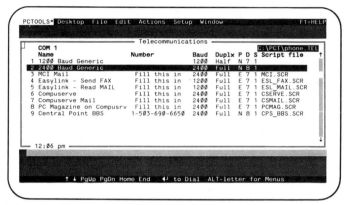

Figure 17.8: The Telecommunications command

The data can be transmitted at a rate of 19,200 baud over one of the serial ports either by character (ASCII) or in blocks (XMODEM). This way, you can even download programs from electronic bulletin boards.

The COMPRESS program lets you combine sectors of files that are scattered on different parts of the disk. Once the sectors are combined, they are written to the hard disk in sequence. This procedure significantly reduces the amount of time necessary to load files. The COMPRESS program is shown in Figure 17.9.

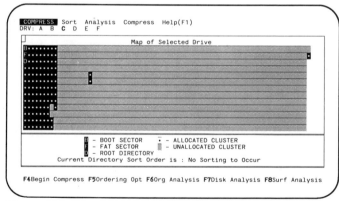

Figure 17.9: The COMPRESS program

The MEMORY INFO program gives you information about the programs resident in memory. Each program's name, memory address, and number of bytes required are listed, as in Figure 17.10.

```
C:\PCT>mi

Memory Info v5.19
Copyright 1989 Central Point Software, Inc.  All rights reserved.

Conventional memory, Total:   640k
Largest executable program:   444k

Type  Paragraphs  Bytes   Owner
----  ----------  -----   -----------
Prog  13BA-148Ch   3376   13BAh <itself>
Prog  14ED-24DFh  65328   14EDh <itself> C:\PCT\PC-CACHE.COM
Prog  24EE-26D4h   7792   24EEh <itself> c:\util\IMCAP.COM
Prog  26E3-3109h  41584   26E3h <itself> C:\PCT\DESKTOP.EXE/R/CS
Prog  3118-9FFFh   444k   3118h <itself> C:\PCT\MI.COM

Extended (AT/286/386) memory.  Apparent size: 1024k

C:\PCT>
```

Figure 17.10: The MEMORY INFO program

The PC-CACHE program is especially worth noting. It builds a software-driven memory cache. The size of the memory cache is limited solely by the amount of available memory—a 16-megabyte memory cache is the largest that can be managed by the program.

PC-CACHE increases the data transfer rate many times over. A hard-disk system with a data transfer rate of 248 kilobytes can achieve a data transfer rate of almost 3000 kilobytes when PC-CACHE is added. This program alone justifies the purchase of the entire PC Tools Deluxe software package. Figure 17.11 shows the PC-CACHE opening screen.

Norton Utilities Advanced Version

The Norton Utilities advanced version provides many useful programs to help you out of a number of situations. For example, you can search for character strings, edit the file allocation table (FAT), and edit any directory or system area.

```
C:\PCT>pc-cache

PC-CACHE, Version 5.1
Unauthorized duplication prohibited.
PC-CACHE has been set up as follows:

        Perform batch copies to/from cache.
        Read a maximu  of  4 sectors ahead.
        256K Extended memory cache at  2176K has been set up as follows:
                        Conventional        Extended
        DOS/Resid nt        203K                 0K
        PC-CACHE             14K               256K
        Available          423K              1152K
        Total              640K              1408K

    PC-CACHE program successfully installed.
    Specify /? for information on parameters.

C:\PCT>
```

Figure 17.11: The PC-CACHE opening screen

With the disk editor, you can access a specific sector, a specific cluster, or a previously specified file. Figure 17.12 shows the opening menu of the Norton Utilities Advanced Version.

Sorting directories

With the DS (Directory Sort) program, which is shown in Figure 17.13, you can sort the files in your directory according to various criteria. You can sort the files alphabetically, by name, by size, date, time, or file name extension.

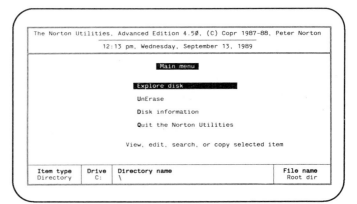

Figure 17.12: The Norton Utilities Advanced Version opening menu

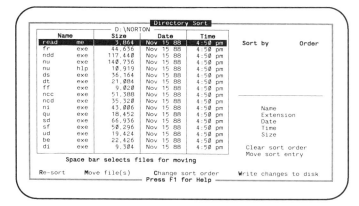

Figure 17.13: The Norton Utilities Directory Sort program

You use the SD (Speed Disk) program to combine file sectors scattered across the disk. Once the files are combined, they are written to the hard disk in sequence. This makes file loading go much faster. Figure 17.14 shows the Speed Disk program at work.

A file you have accidentally erased is lost forever under normal circumstances. Still, the QU (Quick Unerase) program allows you to reconstruct the unintentionally erased files. You will learn very quickly to appreciate this program. It is especially useful when you have erased a program for which you have no backup copy.

Recalling erased files

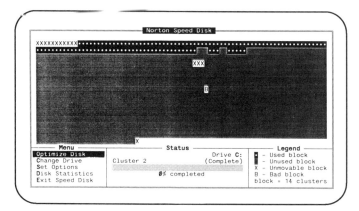

Figure 17.14: The Norton Utilities Speed Disk program

You can obtain technical information about your computer system with the SI (System Information) program. The values reported from this program—CI (Computing Index), DI (Disk Index), and PI (Performance Index)—give information about the performance of your computer system. Figure 17.15 shows a readout obtained from the System Information program.

You can extract technical information about the division of a hard disk with the DI (Disk Information) program, as shown in Figure 17.16.

```
              Computer Name: IBM AT
           Operating System: DOS 3.30
          Built-in BIOS dated: Tuesday, April 14, 1987
             Main Processor: Intel 80286              Serial Ports: 1
               Co-Processor: None                    Parallel Ports: 1
      Video Display Adapter: Enhanced Graphics (EGA), 256 K-bytes
          Current Video Mode: Text, 80 x 25 Monochrome
      Available Disk Drives: 6, A: - F:

      DOS reports 640 K-bytes of memory:
        274 K-bytes used by DOS and resident programs
        366 K-bytes available for application programs
      A search for active memory finds:
        640 K-bytes main memory     (at hex 0000-0A000)
         32 K-bytes display memory  (at hex 0B000-0B800)
      1,024 K-bytes extended memory (at hex 10000-20000)
      ROM-BIOS Extensions are found at hex paragraphs: C000

      Computing Index (CI), relative to IBM/XT: 10.4
         Disk Index (DI), relative to IBM/XT: 6.8

      Performance Index (PI), relative to IBM/XT: 9.2

      D:\NORTON>
```

Figure 17.15: The Norton Utilities System Information program

```
      D:\NORTON>di
      DI-Disk Information, Advanced Edition 4.50, (C) Copr 1987-88, Peter Norton

          Information from DOS         Drive D:       Information from the boot record
      ---------------------------------------------------------------------------------
                                 system id          'IBM 3.3'
                                 media descriptor (hex)        F8
                3                drive number
              512                bytes per sector              512
                4                sectors per cluster             4
                2                number of FATs                  2
              512                root directory entries        512
               45                sectors per FAT                45
           11,363               number of clusters
                                 number of sectors         45,577
                1               offset to FAT                   1
               91               offset to directory
              123               offset to data
                                 sectors per track             17
                                 sides                          9
                                 hidden sectors                17

      D:\NORTON>
```

Figure 17.16: The Norton Utilities Disk Information program

A hard disk you've accidentally formatted can be restored with the FR (Format Recover) program. To use this program, however, you must have stored the corresponding system information beforehand with the SAVE option of the same command. Figure 17.17 shows the Norton Utilities Format Recover program.

In order to keep from accidentally erasing your files, you can set the files' read-only attribute with the FA (File Attributes) program, which is shown in Figure 17.18.

Other attributes can be changed with this program as well. For example, you can change screen attributes—for instance, the

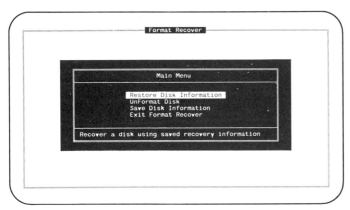

Figure 17.17: Norton Utilities Format Recover program

```
D:\>fa
FA-File Attributes, Advanced Edition 4.50, (C) Copr 1987-88, Peter Norton

D:\
    frecover.dat   Archive Read-only
    frecover.bak   Archive Read-only
    frecover.idx   Archive Read-only Hidden System
    sd.ini
    part
    qd2.log
    green          Archive

    7 files shown
    0 files changed

D:\>
```

Figure 17.18: The Norton Utilities File Attributes program

foreground and background color—with the Norton Control Center.

The FI (File Info) program, shown in Figure 17.19, represents quite a great help also. This program provides a short description of each file. For example, if you are looking for a specific file whose name you can't remember, the brief description will certainly help you find it.

```
D:\NORTON>fi f*.*
FI-File Info, Advanced Edition 4.50, (C) Copr 1987-88, Peter Norton

  Directory of D:\NORTON

  fr         exe      44,636   11-15-88   4:50p   Recover accidentally formatted disk
  ff         exe       9,020   11-15-88   4:50p   Find lost files and directories
  fa         exe       9,304   11-15-88   4:50p   Set, reset, and scan file attributes
  fd         exe      10,294   11-15 88   4:50p   Set a file's date and time stamp
  fi         exe      18,438   11-15-88   4:50p   Attach and view filename comments
  fs         exe       9,218   11-15-88   4:50p   List or total file sizes
  fileinfo fi          3,217   11-15-88   4:50p   Contains all of the file comments
  format!    exe      50,296   11 15 88   4:50p

  8 files found       3,645,440 bytes free

D:\NORTON>
```

Figure 17.19: The Norton Utilities File Info program

The computer makes music

The BEEP program was made with the musically inclined user in mind. A short melody or even an entire song can be played. The frequency and length of the notes can be set directly. Repetitions and rests are possible too. Usually the BEEP program is used to announce that a batch file's operation has ended.

Besides the programs just described, the Norton Utilities offers other programs that address various problems.

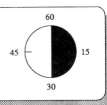
RAM Disks

RAM Disks

As the name suggests, a RAM disk is similar to a diskette or hard disk. The difference is that RAM disks are also addressed by way of their drive letter designations. DOS commands such as COPY or XCOPY are used on a RAM disk the same way they are used on a hard disk or diskette.

There are two ways to install a RAM disk. The first is to use a special RAM disk card. Some of these cards even contain battery-powered backups to ensure that data residing on the RAM disk won't be lost after you turn off the computer.

The second way consists of using a portion of the computer's main memory as a RAM disk. A software solution in the form of a special device driver is already included in your DOS operating system. This device driver is called VDISK.SYS on PC-DOS systems. It is called RAMDRIVE.SYS on MS-DOS systems.

VDISK.SYS

VDISK is an abbreviation for the term "virtual disk." This device driver from IBM is easy to install. Insert the following line in your CONFIG.SYS file with your text editor (for example, EDLIN):

```
DEVICE=C:\DOS\VDISK.SYS 1408 512 256 /E:8
```

Below is an explanation of this program line.

DEVICE=: The device driver assignment.

C:\DOS\: The drive and the path from which the device driver should be loaded. VDISK.SYS is the name of the device driver.

`1408:`	The size in kilobytes of the RAM disk to be created. In the example, 1408 kilobytes of memory above 1 megabyte is assumed.
`512:`	The sector size in bytes to be used. Possible values are 128, 256, and 512. The default value is 128.
`256:`	The number of entries in the directory. It can be between 2 and 512. The default value is 64.
`/E8:`	The number, 8 in this case, of sectors that can be transmitted from the RAM disk to the DOS buffer (BUFFERS) at one time. Values from 1 through 8 are allowed. The default value is 8. The /E designation is optional. It may only be used in connection with the extended memory above 1 megabyte.

Use great care when you designate the size of the RAM disk you are creating. For example, a RAM disk of 600 kilobytes cannot be created on a computer with 640 kilobytes of main memory.

At best, you will receive the message "Configuration too large for memory," or the computer may simply freeze if the RAM disk you try to create is too large.

In such a case, there is nothing for you to do but reboot the system from a diskette and edit the CONFIG.SYS file. Booting from the hard disk is not possible, since you cannot interrupt the device driver when it is loading.

Unlike a diskette, the RAM disk needs no explicit formatting. The device driver takes care of the necessary formatting while the disk is being loaded.

When the RAM disk is successfully installed, all the settings are displayed on the screen—the RAM disk is now bound to the system.

The RAM-disk device driver from IBM looks like the screen shown in Figure 18.1.

```
VDISK Version 3.30 virtual disk D:
   Buffer size:        1408 KB
   Sector size:         512
   Directory entries:   256
   Transfer s ze:         8

C:\>
```

Figure 18.1: Report of the VDISK device driver

RAMDRIVE.SYS

The device driver from Microsoft is called RAMDRIVE.SYS. Installing the driver is the same as installing VDISK.SYS, but with one difference: the number of sectors designation, which appears after the /E option, is not available.

The RAMDRIVE.SYS RAM-disk device driver informs you about the composition of the installed RAM disk. Figure 18.2 shows such a report.

```
Microsoft RAMDrive version 2.01 virtual disk D:
   Disk size: 40k
   Sector size: 128 bytes
   Allocation unit: 1 sectors
   Directory entries: 128

C:\>
```

Figure 18.2: Report of the RAMDrive device driver

Copy frequently used utilities right after you've started onto a RAM disk. At this time it is important that utility programs are loaded from the hard disk as soon as they are called up.

In order to bring this about, you must establish a branch of the RAM disk with the DOS PATH command. A command call in the AUTOEXEC.BAT file would look like this:

```
PATH=D:\;C:\;
COPY C:\DOS\*.* D:\
SET COMSPEC=D:\COMMAND.COM
```

This command instructs the operating system to look in the root directory of drive D (in this case, the RAM disk) when a utility is called up that is not in the current directory.

If the utility is located there, it will be loaded from the RAM disk into memory and started. This loading procedure is carried out much faster than it would take the utility to load from the hard disk.

So that the COMMAND.COM command interpreter can also be loaded from the RAM disk, you must enter the SET COMSPEC=D:\COMMAND.COM command.

The advantages of a RAM disk are obvious: it takes advantage of any available memory above 1 megabyte and therefore memory isn't left unused.

The access of semiconductor memory takes less time than a comparable access of a hard disk or diskette. Still, a RAM disk has disadvantages. When you turn off the computer's power, the entire contents of the RAM disk are lost, unless of course the RAM disk has a battery.

 Don't forget to copy files modified on a RAM disk to a non-volatile storage medium such as your hard disk drive. Only copy the utility programs of your operating system, such as FORMAT, EDLIN, etc., onto a RAM disk.

Memory Caches

The memory cache has gained in popularity lately. Technically, it is a segment of memory with a size on the order of 64 kilobytes. The difference between a memory cache and normal memory is its extremely short access time. Normal memory chips, as you use them in the computer, have an access time of about 120 ns, but the memory chips used for memory caches have an access time of only 25 ns. With special hardware conceived for a memory cache, all hard disk and diskette accesses can take place over the memory cache. This procedure is called a hardware cache.

Yet cache memory can be set up without special hardware. A program for this purpose regulates which data must be located in the memory cache.

In contrast to the hardware caches described above, there is also a software cache. The more carefully thought out the cache program is that stores this data in memory, the more effective the introduction of a memory cache is.

Software caches

For instance, suppose the controlling software program were so unintelligent that it was not selective about the data stored in the memory cache. In this case, the constant loading of data into the memory cache from the hard disk would be even slower than accessing the data directly from the hard disk.

Software-cache programs have names like PC-CACHE, LIGHTNIN, or simply CACHE. (Figure 18.3 shows the PC-CACHE informational screen.) These programs take advantage of the otherwise seldom-used memory area above 1 megabyte. With a program like CORETEST, the resulting increase in speed can be easily demonstrated.

Figure 18.4 shows the data reported by CORETEST without a cache program, and Figure 18.5 shows the results of the same computer system with the cache program LIGHTNIN.

There are also hard disk systems with integrated memory caches. Data Pac from Tandon belongs to this group. Data Pac already comes with a memory cache of 64 kilobytes as an interim buffer.

```
C:\PCT>pc-cache

  PC-CACHE, Version 5.1
  Unauthorized duplication prohibited.
  PC-CACHE has been set up as follows:

    Perform batch copies to/from cache.
    Read a maximum of  4 sectors ahead.
    256K Extended memory cache at  2176K has been set up as follows:
                        Conventional      Extended
      DOS/Resident        203K               0K
      PC-CACHE             14K             256K
      Available           423K            1152K
      Total               640K            1408K

  PC-CACHE program successfully installed.
  Specify /? for information on parameters.

C:\PCT>
```

Figure 18.3: PC-CACHE informational screen

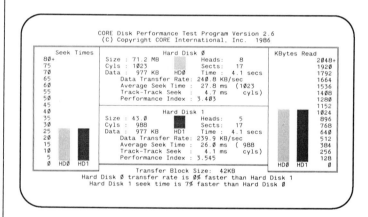

Figure 18.4: CORETEST results without a cache program

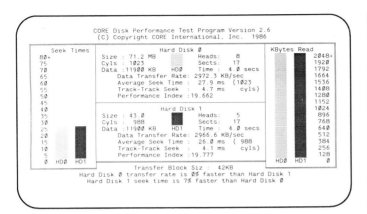

Figure 18.5: CORETEST results with LIGHTNIN in the background

Changing the Operating System

Changing the operating system involves some basic work. First, use either your own DOS version or a third-party program like BACK-IT to make a backup copy of your hard disk. In the case of DOS, use the BACKUP command. However, the root directory, including COMMAND.COM, should not be backed up.

The syntax for the DOS BACKUP program runs as follows:

```
BACKUP Source_file(s) Target_drive/Options
```

Below is an explanation of the parts of the syntax.

Source_file   The pathname, including the drive designation and possibly more exact specifications, of the files to be backed up.

Target_drive   The drive onto which the data is to be backed up.

/Options   The options for the manner in which the data is to be backed up.

Table 19.1 shows the various options of the DOS BACKUP program and their functions.

Option	Effect
/A	Old backup files are not erased. A new backup file will be added.

Table 19.1: Options available with the BACKUP command

Option	Effect
/D	Only files created or modified after the specified date are backed up.
/F	The target diskette is formatted if necessary.
/L	A log file is produced for the backup procedure.
/M	Only modified files are backed up.
/S	All files that are located in subdirectories of the selected directory are backed up.
/T	Only files created or modified after the specified time are backed up.

Table 19.1: Options available with the BACKUP command (cont.)

Consider the example below.

```
C>backup c:\dos a: /d:10/03/87
```

This tells DOS to back up all files located in the DOS sub-directory on drive C that were created after October 3rd, 1987 onto the diskette in drive A.

Using the BACKUP command to perform the data backup takes quite some time. Besides backing up your data, you should copy the previous operating system, including the utility programs FORMAT, FDISK, BACKUP, and RESTORE, to one or two diskettes. Furthermore, make certain that the previous operating system can be loaded from a diskette. Go through the necessary steps before you proceed with the next step.

Deleting partitions

Now use the DOS FDISK utility to delete the partitions that have up till now been reserved for your operating system. This is the safest way to signal to the new operating system that you have an empty hard disk.

Next you can install the new operating system onto the hard disk, as described in Steps 9–12.

After you've finished installing the new operating system, start your computer with the previous operating system. Here you should use one of the diskettes.

With the DOS RESTORE program from the previous DOS version, you can now restore your data back onto the hard disk.

The syntax for the DOS RESTORE program runs as follows:

```
RESTORE Backup_drive Target_drive
```

Below is an explanation of this syntax.

`Backup_drive`   The drive on which the diskette produced with the BACKUP command is located.

`Target_drive`   The drive whose data should be restored.

Backup drive and target drive are specified by using their drive designations.

Example:

```
A>RESTORE A: C:
```

The next boot of the computer can now be made successfully with the new operating system.

For more information about the DOS BACKUP and RE-STORE programs, consult your DOS handbook.

What the Future Has in Store

In the future there will be even more innovations in the realm of mass storage media.

For example, the Verbatim company offers a diskette drive with a 10- or even 20-megabyte storage capacity, an average access time of 65 microseconds, and an SCSI interface. The data transfer rate with these diskette drives amounts to 2 megabits per second. In addition, they possess an internal 16-kilobyte memory buffer.

20-mega-byte disk drive

To guarantee a high reliability of data storage, the diskettes come preformatted from the factory with track information.

Track informa-tion

In operation, the track information is used to test and correct the middle position of the read/write head 78 times per second if need be. Instead of stepper motor actuators, faster and more precise voice coil actuators are used.

Because the outermost tracks of a diskette are longer than the inner tracks, the data on the outlying tracks is recorded in a correspondingly denser format. With the 10-megabyte version, the disks have a track density of 333 tpi (tracks per inch). Figure 20.1 shows the Verbatim diskette drive with a capacity of 10 megabytes.

In comparison, normal high-density diskettes, like those used with 1.2-megabyte disk drives, have a track density of 96 tpi. With this extremely dense recording, the bit density amounts to 19,968 bpi (bits per inch).

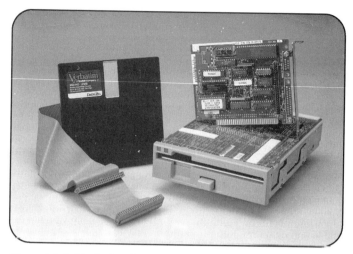

Figure 20.1: Verbatim diskette drive with a capacity of 10 megabytes

The diskettes used have the 5.25-inch format. In order to offer additional protection against damage, they are housed in a hard plastic casing.

Two write-protect zones in the diskette make it possible to store application software and data separately. This reduces the danger of writing over applications with data.

CD-ROM Drives

Special device drivers

Also gaining in importance are special CD-ROM drives. Sony offers such a drive under the name CDU-510-01 at a cost of $1000. The CD drive is connected to its own controller (CDB-230).

With a special device driver, the drive can be addressed quite normally under DOS. A single disk with this drive has a storage capacity of 660 megabytes.

Right now CD-ROM drives are too expensive for most people. Besides, the software needed to drive the CD-ROM drives is not yet standardized, so for the time being it is not advisable to install such a disk drive.

Index

DI (Disk Index) program (Norton
    Utilities), 100
DIAG diagnostic program, 42
DIP switches, 8
directory, in prompt command, 88
DIRECTORY command (PC Tools De-
    luxe), 91
Directory Sort (DS) program (Norton Utili-
    ties), 98
disk capacity, in Advanced RLL en-
    coding, 17
disk card, RAM, 103
Disk Index (DI) program (Norton
    Utilities), 100
DISK MANAGER (Ontrack), 32, 42–47
    and hard disk capacity, 59
    starting, 42–43
DISKCOPY command (DOS), 32
diskette drives
    high-density, 2
    rotation of, 4
diskettes
    for data backup, 81
    high-density, 115
    working, from DOS 4.0, 73
DMDRVR.BIN device driver, 42
documentation, v
dollar sign ($) prefix, 87
DOS
    hard disk partition for, 55
    installing, through 3.2x, 59–62
    two hard disks under, 79
    version, in prompt command, 88
DOS 3.3, installing, 63–70
DOS 4.0
    creating working diskette by, 73
    file allocation table for, 56
    installing, 71–73
    manually installing, 73
    user shell in, 72
DOS commands, 85–89
    BACKUP, 81, 111–112
    BUFFERS, 85
    CHKDSK, 22
    DISKCOPY, 32
    FDISK, 48, 55, 59–68, 112
    FILES, 85
    FORMAT, 61, 68–69
        vs. PC Tools Deluxe
        PCFORMAT, 91
    PATH, 85–86

RAM disk in, 106
PROMPT, 86–88
RESTORE, 81, 113
SET, 88–89
VDISK.SYS, 103–105
VER command, 88–89
DOS hidden files, 61
DOS partition
    creating, 59
    formatting, 61, 68–69
DOS programs
    under OS/2, 75
    under UNIX, 77
DOS subdirectory, 62
downloading programs, from electronic bul-
    letin boards, 96
driver cards, and backup speed, 83
drives. See also hard disks
    asynchronous and synchronous, 13
    logical, 55, 63, 67
    specifying in prompt, 86
DS (Directory Sort) program (Norton
    Utilities), 98

E

editor
    in Norton Utilities, 98
    in PC Tools Deluxe, 92
electric current, and parked head, 5
electrical connections, checking, 39
electronic bulletin boards, downloading
    programs from, 96
encoding, data, 15–18
encoding schemes, 3–4
equal sign (=), in prompt command, 88
erased files, restoring, 91
error correction, 16–17
error messages
    in boot record, 56
    after installing XT hard disk controller, 39
"Error reading drive" message, 22
escape key, 67
    in prompt command, 87
ESDI (enhanced small device) interface, 3,
    7, 11–12
    installing, 36–38
    maximum sectors per track for, 16
ESDI controllers, 28
    interleave factor for, 40
    SpeedStor and, 47
.EXE extension files, 86

Expanded Diagnostics Diskette (IBM), 24
extended memory, VDISK in, 104
extended partitions, 63, 66–68
external hard disks, 20
external tape backup device, 83

F

FA (Files Attributes) program (Norton
    Utilities), 101
FastBack (Fifth Generation Systems), 82
FastBack Plus (Fifth Generation
    Systems), 82
FAT (file allocation table), 4, 56–57
FDISK command (DOS), 48, 55, 59–62
    to create extended partitions, 66–68
    to delete partitions, 112
FDISK command (DOS 3.3), 63–66
FI (File Info) program, 102
Fifth Generation Systems
    FastBack, 82
    FastBack Plus, 82
file allocation table (FAT), 56–57 damage
    to, 4
File Info (FI) program, 102
files
    accidentally erased, 91, 99, 101
    backing up, 5, 32, 82–83
    maximum number of addressable, 85
    scattered sectors, 96, 99
    sorting with Norton Utilities, 98
    system, 56
FILES command (DOS), 85
Flashback (Overland Data), 82
floppy disk drives
    high-density, 2
    rotation, 4
floppy disks, and hard disk designation, 79
flux density, 15
flux reversal, 15
FORMAT command (DOS), 61,
    68–69
    vs. PCTools Deluxe PCFORMAT, 91
Format Recover (FR) program (Norton
    Utilities), 101
formatting
    DOS partition, 61, 68–69
    low-level, 22, 39
    RAM disk, 104
    recovery from accidental, 101
FR (Format Recover) program (Norton
    Utilities), 101

full-height 5.25 hard disks, dimensions, 20

G

Gazelle Systems, Back-It program, 81
guarantee, from manufacturers, 6
guaranteed minimum capacity, 22

H

half-height 5.25 hard disks, dimensions, 20
handling, of hard disks, 34
hard disks
    access to, and light diode, 38
    accidental formatting, 101
    capacity. See storage capacity
    construction, 20
    differences, 1
    dimensions, 1, 20
    handling, 34
    installing second, 19
    minimum capacity, for UNIX, 77–78
    mounting location for, 35
    number assigned to, 8
    opening housing, 6
    parts, 3
    plug-in, 20
    purchasing used, 21
    selection, 8, 19–22
    similarities in, 1–2
    speed, 4
    systems with two, under DOS, 79
HARDPREP program (SpeedStor), 48
hardware cache, 107
heads, 1
    lifting, 5–6
    parking, 4–5
help, from Back-It program, 82
Help function, in DOS 4.0, 72
hidden files, DOS, 61
high-density diskettes, 115
high-density floppy disk drives, 2
host adapter, controllers for SCSI interface
    system with, 29

I

IBM Expanded Diagnostics Diskette, 24
IBM PS/2 computers, controllers for, 25
IBMBIO.COM file, 56, 61
IBMDOS.COM file, 56, 61
image backup, 82–83
initialization, 39–53

data loss from, 51
installation, 35–38
installation software, 32
integrated memory caches, 108
interfaces, 1, 7–8
and controller selection, 23
interleave, 10–11, 40–41
in initialization, 46
for SpeedStor, 50
IO.SYS system file, 56

J

jumpers, 8, 35–36
settings for, 42

K

key lock, 35
kilobytes, 2
knocking, 4

L

landing zone location, for initialization program, 41
less than character (<), in prompt command, 88
letter designations, for multiple hard disks, 79
light diode, for hard disk access, 38
LIGHTNIN, 107
LOCATE command (PC Tools Deluxe), 91
location, for mounting, 34
log file, during backup, 112
logical drives, 55, 67
on extended partitions, 63
formatting, 69
logical sectors, and physical, 40–41
low-level formatting, 22, 39
LPT 1, as printer port designation, 72

M

manual installation, of DOS 4.0, 73
manufacturer's guarantee, 6
mass storage, innovations in, 115
megabyte capacity, determining, 2
memory
CMOS RAM, 24, 43
extended, VDISK in, 104
file allocation table in, 57
for OS/2, 75
programs resident in, 97

as RAM disk, 103
for UNIX, 77
vs. memory cache, 107
memory caches, 107–109
integrated, 108
memory chips, access time of, 107
MEMORY INFO program (PC Tools Deluxe), 97
messages. *See* error messages
MFM (modified frequency modulation) encoding, 3, 6–7,15–16, 18, 21
hard disk drive with, 44
maximum transfer rate of, 10
with ST506/412 interface, controller for, 26
microchannel architecture, 25
controller for, 27–28
Micropolis hard disk, 49
Microsoft, RAMDRIVE.SYS,105–106
minimum capacity, guaranteed, 22
MODEL CODE prompt, in DISK MANAGER, 43
modified frequency modulation (MFM) encoding. *See* MFM (modified frequency modulation) encoding
mounting location, 34
for hard disk, 35
mounting materials, 32
mounting rails, 37
MSDOS.SYS system file, 56
multiple devices, with SCSI interface, 12
multiuser system, UNIX as, 77
music, from BEEP program (Norton Utilities), 102

N

Norton Utilities Advanced Version, 97–102
BEEP program in, 102
recovering erased files with, 99
system technical information from, 100
NOTEPAD command (PC Tools Deluxe), 93
numbering, of tracks, 2

O

older personal computers, hard disks for, 20
Ontrack Computer Systems, DISK MANAGER program, 32, 42–47
operating system, 5, 32
changing, 111–113
determining version, 88

disk loaded from, 61
loading, 65
partition table and, 55
in primary partition, 63
OS/2
hard disk partition for, 55
installing, 75

P

park cylinder, 4
for initialization program, 41
park track, 4
parking process, for head, 4–5
partition table, 55
partitions, 55–57
deleting with FDISK, 112
DOS, 59
maximum size, 55
for OS/2, 75
and SpeedStor, 48
types, 63
for UNIX operating system, 77
PATH command (DOS), 85–86, 88
RAM disk in, 106
path statements, length, 86
PC Tools Deluxe (Central Point Software),
82, 91–97
appointment calendar in, 93–94
CALCULATOR command in, 95
COMPRESS program, 96
DATABASE command in, 94
DESKTOP program, 93
MEMORY INFO program, 97
NOTEPAD command, 93
PC-CACHE program in, 97, 107–108
PCBACKUP, 92
PCFORMAT program, 91
PCSETUP program, 91
PCSHELL program, 91–92
telecommunications command in, 95–96
Pdisk (Phoenix Technologies), 82
Performance Index (PI) program (Norton
Utilities), 100
peripherals, communication of computer
with, 5
personal computers, older, hard disks for, 20
physical sectors, and logical, 40–41
PI (Performance Index) program (Norton
Utilities), 100
pin 1
on controller card, 36

identification, 8
platters, 1
plug-in hard disks, 20
polarity guard, 31
power connectors, 31
power fork cable, 31
power supply, 31, 38
predefined character sequences, for
prompts, 87
primary partitions, 63–65
PRINT command (PC Tools Deluxe), 91
printer port, designating, 72
printer selection, in DOS 4.0 installation, 72
programs. *See also* specific programs
downloading from electronic bulletin
boards, 96
for head parking, 4–5
installing, 32
storage, 19
PROMPT command (DOS), 86–88
prompts, predefined character sequences
for, 87

Q

QIC-11 recording procedures, 83
QIC-24 recording procedures, 83
Quick Unerase (QU) program (Norton
Utilities), 99

R

rails, mounting, 37
RAM. *See also* memory
CMOS, 24
RAM disks, 79, 103–109
size, 104
RAMDRIVE.SYS (Microsoft), 103,
105–106
read-only attribute, of files, 101
read/write head, 1
rebooting, 44–45, 65
keys, 73
reduced write current, 20–21
and initialization program, 41
reserve wattage, 31
resistor circuits, 7, 14
resistors, terminating, 7, 14, 36
RESTORE program (DOS), 81, 113
RLL controllers, SpeedStor and, 47
RLL encoding, 3, 6–7, 16–18

used hard disks, purchasing, 21
utilities, 91–102
    on RAM disk, 106

V

VDISK.SYS (DOS), 103–105
VER command (DOS), 88, 89
Verbatim Company, 115
vertical character (|), in prompt, 87
virtual disk, 103
voice coil actuators, 115

W

wattage, reserve, 31
Western Digital
    WD1006V-MC1 controller, 25

WD1007V-MC1 controller, 25
whirring sound, 5
windows, from PCSHELL, 92
working diskette, DOS 4.0 creating, 73
write current, reduced, 20–21, 41
write pre-compensation, 21
    and initialization program, 42
write-protect zones, 116

X

XMODEM, 96
XT computers
    controller for, 23, 26–28, 36, 39–42
    installing hard disk on, 32
    interleave value for, 40
XT-GEN Dynamic Formatter initialization
    program, 39–40

Selections from
The SYBEX Library

DOS

The ABC's of DOS 4
Alan R. Miller
275pp. Ref. 583-2
This step-by-step introduction to using DOS 4 is written especially for beginners. Filled with simple examples, *The ABC's of DOS 4* covers the basics of hardware, software, disks, the system editor EDLIN, DOS commands, and more.

ABC's of MS-DOS
(Second Edition)
Alan R. Miller
233pp. Ref. 493-3
This handy guide to MS-DOS is all many PC users need to manage their computer files, organize floppy and hard disks, use EDLIN, and keep their computers organized. Additional information is given about utilities like Sidekick, and there is a DOS command and program summary. The second edition is fully updated for Version 3.3.

Mastering DOS
(Second Edition)
Judd Robbins
722pp. Ref. 555-7
"The most useful DOS book." This seven-part, in-depth tutorial addresses the needs of users at all levels. Topics range from running applications, to managing files and directories, configuring the system, batch file programming, and techniques for system developers. Through Version 4.

Understanding DOS 3.3
Judd Robbins
678pp. Ref. 648-0
This best selling, in-depth tutorial addresses the needs of users at all levels with many examples and hands-on exercises. Robbins discusses the fundamentals of DOS, then covers manipulating files and directories, using the DOS editor, printing, communicating, and finishes with a full section on batch files.

MS-DOS Handbook
(Third Edition)
Richard Allen King
362pp. Ref. 492-5
This classic has been fully expanded and revised to include the latest features of MS-DOS Version 3.3. Two reference books in one, this title has separate sections for programmer and user. Multi-DOS partitons, 3 1/2-inch disk format, batch file call and return feature, and comprehensive coverage of MS-DOS commands are included. Through Version 3.3.

MS-DOS Power User's Guide,
Volume I
(Second Edition)
Jonathan Kamin
482pp. Ref. 473-9
A fully revised, expanded edition of our best-selling guide to high-performance DOS techniques and utilities—with details on Version 3.3. Configuration, I/O, directory structures, hard disks, RAM disks, batch file programming, the ANSI.SYS device driver, more. Through Version 3.3.

MS-DOS Power User's Guide,
Volume II
Martin Waterhouse/Jonathan Kamin
418pp, Ref. 411-9
A second volume of high-performance techniques and utilities, with expanded coverage of DOS 3.3, and new material on video modes, Token-Ring and PC Network support, micro-mainframe links, extended and expanded memory, multitasking systems, and more. Through Version 3.3.

DOS User's Desktop Companion
SYBEX Ready Reference Series
Judd Robbins
969 pp. Ref. 505-0
This comprehensive reference covers DOS commands, batch files, memory enhancements, printing, communications and more information on optimizing each user's DOS environment. Written with step-by-step instructions and plenty of examples, this volume covers all versions through 3.3.

MS-DOS Advanced
Programming
Michael J. Young
490pp. Ref. 578-6
Practical techniques for maximizing performance in MS-DOS software by making best use of system resources. Topics include functions, interrupts, devices, multitasking, memory residency and more, with examples in C and assembler. Through Version 3.3.

Essential PC-DOS
(Second Edition)
Myril Clement Shaw
Susan Soltis Shaw
332pp. Ref. 413-5
An authoritative guide to PC-DOS, including version 3.2. Designed to make experts out of beginners, it explores everything from disk management to batch file programming. Includes an 85-page command summary. Through Version 3.2.

The IBM PC-DOS Handbook
(Third Edition)
Richard Allen King
359pp. Ref. 512-3
A guide to the inner workings of PC-DOS 3.2, for intermediate to advanced users and programmers of the IBM PC series. Topics include disk, screen and port control, batch files, networks, compatibility, and more. Through Version 3.3.

DOS Instant Reference
SYBEX Prompter Series
Greg Harvey/Kay Yarborough Nelson
220pp. Ref. 477-1, 4 ¾" × 8"
A complete fingertip reference for fast, easy on-line help:command summaries, syntax, usage and error messages. Organized by function—system commands, file commands, disk management, directories, batch files, I/O, networking, programming, and more. Through Version 3.3.

Hard Disk Instant Reference
SYBEX Prompter Series
Judd Robbins
256pp. Ref. 587-5, 4 ¾" × 8"
Compact yet comprehensive, this pocket-sized reference presents the essential information on DOS commands used in managing directories and files, and in optimizing disk configuration. Includes a survey of third-party utility capabilities. Through DOS 4.0.

Understanding Hard Disk
Management on the PC
Jonathan Kamin
500pp. Ref. 561-1
This title is a key productivity tool for all hard disk users who want efficient, error-free file management and organization. Includes details on the best ways to conserve hard disk space when using several memory-guzzling programs. Through DOS 4.

UTILITIES

Mastering the Norton Utilities
Peter Dyson
373pp. Ref. 575-1
In-depth descriptions of each Norton utility make this book invaluable for begin-

ning and experienced users alike. Each utility is described clearly with examples and the text is organized so that readers can put Norton to work right away. Version 4.5.

Mastering SideKick Plus
Gene Weisskopf
394pp. Ref. 558-1
Employ all of Sidekick's powerful and expanded features with this hands-on guide to the popular utility. Features include comprehensive and detailed coverage of time management, note taking, outlining, auto dialing, DOS file management, math, and copy-and-paste functions.

COMMUNICATIONS

Mastering Crosstalk XVI
(Second Edition)
Peter W. Gofton
225pp. Ref. 642-1
Introducing the communications program Crosstalk XVI for the IBM PC. As well as providing extensive examples of command and script files for programming Crosstalk, this book includes a detailed description of how to use the program's more advanced features, such as windows, talking to mini or mainframe, customizing the keyboard and answering calls and background mode.

HARDWARE

The RS-232 Solution
(Second Edition)
Joe Campbell
193pp. Ref. 488-7
For anyone wanting to use their computer's serial port, this complete how-to guide is updated and expanded for trouble-free RS-232-C interfacing from scratch. Solution shows you how to connect a variety of computers, printers, and modems, and it includes details for IBM PC AT, PS/2, and Macintosh.

Mastering Serial
Communications
Peter W. Gofton
289pp. Ref. 180-2
The software side of communications, with details on the IBM PC's serial programming, the XMODEM and Kermit protocols, non-ASCII data transfer, interrupt-level programming and more. Sample programs in C, assembly language and BASIC.

Microprocessor Interfacing Techniques (Third Edition)
Austin Lesea/Rodnay Zaks
456pp. Ref. 029-6
This handbook is for engineers and hobbyists alike, covering every aspect of interfacing microprocessors with peripheral devices. Topics include assembling a CPU, basic I/O, analog circuitry, and bus standards.

From Chips to Systems: An Introduction to Microcomputers (Second Edition)
Rodnay Zaks/Alexander Wolfe
580pp. Ref. 377-5
The best-selling introduction to microcomputer hardware—now fully updated, revised, and illustrated. Such recent advances as 32-bit processors and RISC architecture are introduced and explained for the first time in a beginning text.

NETWORKS

The ABC's of Novell Netware
Jeff Woodward
282pp. Ref. 614-6
For users who are new to PC's or networks, this entry-level tutorial outlines each basic element and operation of Novell. The ABC's introduces computer hardware and software, DOS, network organization and security, and printing and communicating over the netware system.

Mastering Novell Netware
Cheryl C. Currid/Craig A. Gillett
500pp. Ref. 630-8
Easy and comprehensive, this book is a thorough guide for System Administrators to installing and operating a microcomputer network using Novell Netware. Mastering covers actually setting up a network from start to finish, design, administration, maintenance, and troubleshooting.

Networking with TOPS
Steven William Rimmer
350pp. Ref. 565-4
A hands on guide to the most popular user friendly network available. This book will walk a user through setting up the hardware and software of a variety of TOPS configurations, from simple two station networks through whole offices. It explains the realities of sharing files between PC compatibles and Macintoshes, of sharing printers and other peripherals and, most important, of the real world performance one can expect when the network is running.

SPREADSHEETS AND INTEGRATED SOFTWARE

Visual Guide to Lotus 1-2-3
Jeff Woodward
250pp. Ref. 641-3
Readers match what they see on the screen with the book's screen-by-screen action sequences. For new Lotus users, topics include computer fundamentals, opening and editing a worksheet, using graphs, macros, and printing typeset-quality reports. For Release 2.2.

The ABC's of 1-2-3 Release 2.2
Chris Gilbert/Laurie Williams
340pp. Ref. 623-5
New Lotus 1-2-3 users delight in this book's step-by-step approach to building trouble-free spreadsheets, displaying graphs, and efficiently building databases. The authors cover the ins and outs of the latest version including easier calculations, file linking, and better graphic presentation.

The ABC's of 1-2-3 Release 3
Judd Robbins
290pp. Ref. 519-0
The ideal book for beginners who are new to Lotus or new to Release 3. This step-by-step approach to the 1-2-3 spreadsheet software gets the reader up and running with spreadsheet, database, graphics, and macro functions.

The ABC's of 1-2-3 (Second Edition)
Chris Gilbert/Laurie Williams
245pp. Ref. 355-4
Online Today recommends it as "an easy and comfortable way to get started with the program." An essential tutorial for novices, it will remain on your desk as a valuable source of ongoing reference and support. For Release 2.

Mastering 1-2-3 (Second Edition)
Carolyn Jorgensen
702pp. Ref. 528-X
Get the most from 1-2-3 Release 2 with this step-by-step guide emphasizing advanced features and practical uses. Topics include data sharing, macros, spreadsheet security, expanded memory, and graphics enhancements.

Mastering 1-2-3 Release 3
Carolyn Jorgensen
682pp. Ref. 517-4
For new Release 3 and experienced

Release 2 users, "Mastering" starts with a basic spreadsheet, then introduces spreadsheet and database commands, functions, and macros, and then tells how to analyze 3D spreadsheets and make high-impact reports and graphs. Lotus add-ons are discussed and Fast Tracks are included.

The Complete Lotus 1-2-3 Release 2.2 Handbook
Greg Harvey
750pp. Ref. 625-1
This comprehensive handbook discusses every 1-2-3 operating with clear instructions and practical tips. This volume especially emphasizes the new improved graphics, high-speed recalculation techniques, and spreadsheet linking available with Release 2.2.

The Complete Lotus 1-2-3 Release 3 Handbook
Greg Harvey
700pp. Ref. 600-6
Everything you ever wanted to know about 1-2-3 is in this definitive handbook. As a Release 3 guide, it features the design and use of 3D worksheets, and improved graphics, along with using Lotus under DOS or OS/2. Problems, exercises, and helpful insights are included.

Lotus 1-2-3 Desktop Companion
SYBEX Ready Reference Series
Greg Harvey
976pp. Ref. 501-8
A full-time consultant, right on your desk. Hundreds of self-contained entries cover every 1-2-3 feature, organized by topic, indexed and cross-referenced, and supplemented by tips, macros and working examples. For Release 2.

Advanced Techniques in Lotus 1-2-3
Peter Antoniak/E. Michael Lunsford
367pp. Ref. 556-5
This guide for experienced users focuses on advanced functions, and techniques for designing menu-driven applications using macros and the Release 2 command language. Interfacing techniques and add-on products are also considered.

Lotus 1-2-3 Tips and Tricks
Gene Weisskopf
396pp. Ref. 454-2
A rare collection of timesavers and tricks for longtime Lotus users. Topics include macros, range names, spreadsheet design, hardware considerations, DOS operations, efficient data analysis, printing, data interchange, applications development, and more.

Lotus 1-2-3 Instant Reference Release 2.2
SYBEX Prompter Series
Greg Harvey/Kay Yarborough Nelson
254pp. Ref. 635-9, 4 ¾" × 8"
The reader gets quick and easy access to any operation in 1-2-3 Version 2.2 in this handy pocket-sized encyclopedia. Organized by menu function, each command and function has a summary description, the exact key sequence, and a discussion of the options.

Lotus 1-2-3 Instant Reference
SYBEX Prompter Series
Greg Harvey/Kay Yarborough Nelson
296pp. Ref. 475-5; 4 ¾" × 8"
Organized information at a glance. When you don't have time to hunt through hundreds of pages of manuals, turn here for a quick reminder: the right key sequence, a brief explanation of a command, or the correct syntax for a specialized function.

Mastering Symphony (Fourth Edition)
Douglas Cobb
857pp. Ref. 494-1
Thoroughly revised to cover all aspects of the major upgrade of Symphony Version 2, this Fourth Edition of Doug Cobb's classic is still "the Symphony bible" to this complex but even more powerful package. All the new features are discussed and placed in context with prior versions so that both new and previous users will benefit from Cobb's insights.

The ABC's of Quattro
Alan Simpson/Douglas J. Wolf
286pp. Ref. 560-3
Especially for users new to spreadsheets, this is an introduction to the basic concepts and a guide to instant productivity through editing and using spreadsheet formulas and functions. Includes how to print out graphs and data for presentation. For Quattro 1.1.

Mastering Quattro
Alan Simpson
576pp. Ref. 514-X
This tutorial covers not only all of Quattro's classic spreadsheet features, but also its added capabilities including extended graphing, modifiable menus, and the macro debugging environment. Simpson brings out how to use all of Quattro's new-generation-spreadsheet capabilities.

Mastering Framework III
Douglas Hergert/Jonathan Kamin
613pp. Ref. 513-1
Thorough, hands-on treatment of the lat-

est Framework release. An outstanding introduction to integrated software applications, with examples for outlining, spreadsheets, word processing, databases, and more; plus an introduction to FRED programming.

The ABC's of Excel on the IBM PC
Douglas Hergert
326pp. Ref. 567-0
This book is a brisk and friendly introduction to the most important features of Microsoft Excel for PC's. This beginner's book discusses worksheets, charts, database operations, and macros, all with hands-on examples. Written for all versions through Version 2.

Mastering Excel on the IBM PC
Carl Townsend
628pp. Ref. 403-8
A complete Excel handbook with step-by-step tutorials, sample applications and an extensive reference section. Topics include worksheet fundamentals, formulas and windows, graphics, database techniques, special features, macros and more.

Excel Instant Reference
SYBEX Prompter Series
William J. Orvis
368pp. Ref.577-8, 4 ¾" × 8"
This pocket-sized reference book contains all of Excel's menu commands, math operations, and macro functions. Quick and easy access to command syntax, usage, arguments, and examples make this Instant Reference a must. Through Version 1.5

Understanding PFS: First Choice
Gerry Litton
489pp. Ref. 568-9
From basic commands to complex features, this complete guide to the popular integrated package is loaded with step-by-step instructions. Lessons cover creating attractive documents, setting up easy-to-use databases, working with spreadsheets and graphics, and smoothly integrating tasks from different First Choice modules. For Version 3.0.

Mastering Enable
Keith D. Bishop
517pp. Ref. 440-2
A comprehensive, practical, hands-on guide to Enable 2.0—integrated word processing, spreadsheet, database management, graphics, and communications—from basic concepts to custom menus, macros and the Enable Procedural Language.

Mastering Q & A (Second Edition)
Greg Harvey
540pp. Ref. 452-6

This hands-on tutorial explores the Q & A Write, File, and Report modules, and the Intelligent Assistant. English-language command processor, macro creation, interfacing with other software, and more, using practical business examples.

Mastering SuperCalc5
Greg Harvey/Mary Beth Andrasak
500pp. Ref. 624-3
This book offers a complete and unintimidating guided tour through each feature. With step-by-step lessons, readers learn about the full capabilities of spreadsheet, graphics, and data management functions. Multiple spreadsheets, linked spreadsheets, 3D graphics, and macros are also discussed.

DATABASE MANAGEMENT

The ABC's of Paradox
Charles Siegel
300pp. Ref.573-5
Easy to understand and use, this introduction is written so that the computer novice can create, edit, and manage complex Paradox databases. This primer is filled with examples of the Paradox 3.0 menu structure.

Mastering Paradox (Fourth Edition)
Alan Simpson
636pp. Ref. 612-X
Best selling author Alan Simpson simplifies all aspects of Paradox for the beginning to intermediate user. The book starts with database basics, covers multiple tables, graphics, custom applications with PAL, and the Personal Programmer. For Version 3.0.

Quick Guide to dBASE: The Visual Approach
David Kolodney
382pp. Ref. 596-4
This illustrated tutorial provides the beginner with a working knowledge of all the basic functions of dBASE IV. Images of each successive dBASE screen tell how to create and modify a database, add, edit, sort and select records, and print custom labels and reports.

The ABC's of dBASE IV
Robert Cowart
338pp. Ref. 531-X
This superb tutorial introduces beginners to the concept of databases and practical dBASE IV applications featuring the new menu-driven interface, the new report writer, and Query by Example.

Understanding dBASE IV
(Special Edition)
Alan Simpson
880pp. Ref. 509-3
This Special Edition is the best introduction to dBASE IV, written by 1 million-reader-strong dBASE expert Alan Simpson. First it gives basic skills for creating and manipulating efficient databases. Then the author explains how to make reports, manage multiple databases, and build applications. Includes Fast Track speed notes.

Mastering dBASE IV
Programming
Carl Townsend
496pp. Ref. 540-9
This task-oriented book introduces structured dBASE IV programming and commands by setting up a general ledger system, an invoice system, and a quota-tion management system. The author carefully explores the unique character of dBASE IV based on his in-depth understanding of the program.

dBASE IV User's
Instant Reference
SYBEX Prompter Series
Alan Simpson
349pp. Ref. 605-7, 4 ¾" × 8"
This handy pocket-sized reference book gives every new dBASE IV user fast and easy access to any dBASE command. Arranged alphabetically and by function, each entry includes a description, exact syntax, an example, and special tips from Alan Simpson.

dBASE IV Programmer's
Instant Reference
SYBEX Prompter Series
Alan Simpson
544pp. Ref.538-7, 4 ¾" × 8"
This comprehensive reference to every dBASE command and function has everything for the dBASE programmer in a compact, pocket-sized book. Fast and easy access to adding data, sorting, performing calculations, managing multiple databases, memory variables and arrays, windows and menus, networking, and much more. Version 1.1.

dBASE IV User's
Desktop Companion
SYBEX Ready Reference Series
Alan Simpson
950pp. Ref. 523-9
This easy-to-use reference provides an exhaustive resource guide to taking full advantage of the powerful non-programming features of the dBASE IV Control Center. This book discusses query by example, custom reports and data entry screens, macros, the application generator, and the dBASE command and programming language.

dBASE IV Programmer's
Reference Guide
SYBEX Ready Reference Series
Alan Simpson
1000pp. Ref. 539-5
This exhaustive seven-part reference for dBASE IV users includes sections on getting started, using menu-driven dBASE, command-driven dBASE, multiuser dBASE, programming in dBASE, common algorithms, and getting the most out of dBASE. Includes Simpson's tips on the best ways to use this completely redesigned and more powerful program.

The ABC's of dBASE III PLUS
Robert Cowart
264pp. Ref. 379-1
The most efficient way to get beginners up and running with dBASE. Every 'how' and 'why' of database management is demonstrated through tutorials and practical dBASE III PLUS applications.

Understanding dBASE III PLUS
Alan Simpson
415pp. Ref. 349-X
A solid sourcebook of training and ongoing support. Everything from creating a first database to command file programming is presented in working examples, with tips and techniques you won't find anywhere else.

Mastering dBASE III PLUS:
A Structured Approach
Carl Townsend
342pp. Ref. 372-4
In-depth treatment of structured programming for custom dBASE solutions. An ideal study and reference guide for applications developers, new and experienced users with an interest in efficient programming.

Also:
Understanding dBASE III
Alan Simpson
300pp. Ref. 267-1

Advanced Techniques
in dBASE III PLUS
Alan Simpson
454pp. Ref. 369-4
A full course in database design and structured programming, with routines for inventory control, accounts receivable, system management, and integrated databases.

Simpson's dBASE Tips and
Tricks (For dBASE III PLUS)
Alan Simpson
420pp. Ref. 383-X
A unique library of techniques and programs shows how creative use of built-in features can solve all your needs—without expensive add-on products or external languages. Spreadsheet functions, graphics, and much more.

dBASE III PLUS Programmer's Reference Guide
SYBEX Ready Reference Series
Alan Simpson

1056pp. Ref. 508-5
Programmers will save untold hours and effort using this comprehensive, well-organized dBASE encyclopedia. Complete technical details on commands and functions, plus scores of often-needed algorithms.

dBASE Instant Reference
SYBEX Prompter Series
Alan Simpson

471pp. Ref. 484-4; 4 ¾" × 8"
Comprehensive information at a glance: a brief explanation of syntax and usage for every dBASE command, with step-by-step instructions and exact keystroke sequences. Commands are grouped by function in twenty precise categories.

Understanding R:BASE
Alan Simpson/Karen Watterson

609pp. Ref.503-4
This is the definitive R:BASE tutorial, for use with either OS/2 or DOS. Hands-on lessons cover every aspect of the software, from creating and using a database, to custom systems. Includes Fast Track speed notes.

Power User's Guide to R:BASE
Alan Simpson/Cheryl Currid/Craig Gillett

446pp. Ref. 354-6
Supercharge your R:BASE applications with this straightforward tutorial that covers system design, structured programming, managing multiple data tables, and more. Sample applications include ready-to-run mailing, inventory and accounts receivable systems. Through Version 2.11.

Understanding Oracle
James T. Perry/Joseph G. Lateer

634pp. Ref. 534-4
A comprehensive guide to the Oracle database management system for administrators, users, and applications developers. Covers everything in Version 5 from database basics to multi-user systems, performance, and development tools including SQL*Forms, SQL*Report, and SQL*Calc. Includes Fast Track speed notes.

SYBEX Computer Books are different.

Here is why . . .

At SYBEX, each book is designed with you in mind. Every manuscript is carefully selected and supervised by our editors, who are themselves computer experts. We publish the best authors, whose technical expertise is matched by an ability to write clearly and to communicate effectively. Programs are thoroughly tested for accuracy by our technical staff. Our computerized production department goes to great lengths to make sure that each book is well-designed.

In the pursuit of timeliness, SYBEX has achieved many publishing firsts. SYBEX was among the first to integrate personal computers used by authors and staff into the publishing process. SYBEX was the first to publish books on the CP/M operating system, microprocessor interfacing techniques, word processing, and many more topics.

Expertise in computers and dedication to the highest quality product have made SYBEX a world leader in computer book publishing. Translated into fourteen languages, SYBEX books have helped millions of people around the world to get the most from their computers. We hope we have helped you, too.

For a complete catalog of our publications:

SYBEX, Inc. 2021 Challenger Drive, #100, Alameda, CA 94501
Tel: (415) 523-8233/(800) 227-2346   Telex: 336311
Fax: (415) 523-2373